My Learning Adventures

USA

San Diego, California

My USA

The state I was born in: ____________________

States I've lived in: ____________________

____

____

____

____

____

The states where members of my family have lived: ____________________

____

____

____

____

____

____

The states where members of my family were born: ____________________

____

____

____

____

____

The states where members of my family live now: ____________________

____

____

____

____

____

Bonus Stickers

Stickers to use on pages 5–70

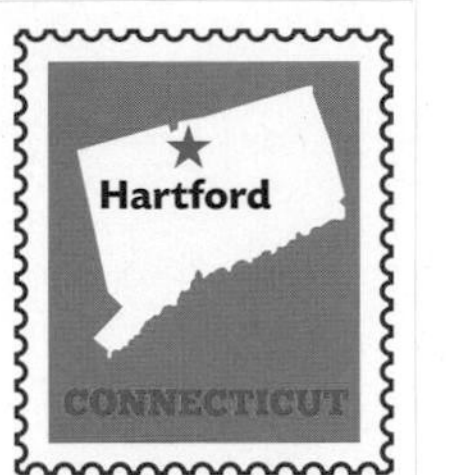

Bismarck
NORTH DAKOTA

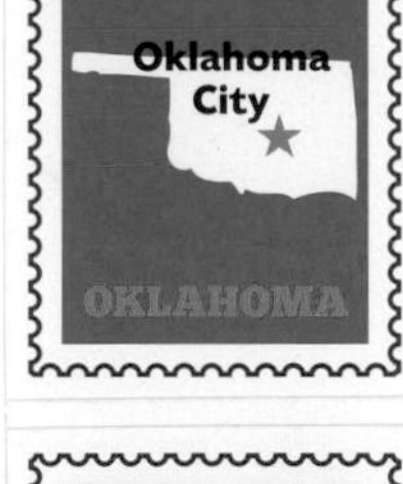

Salem
OREGON

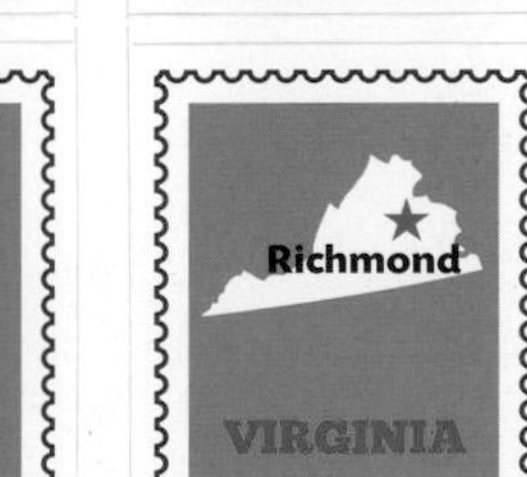

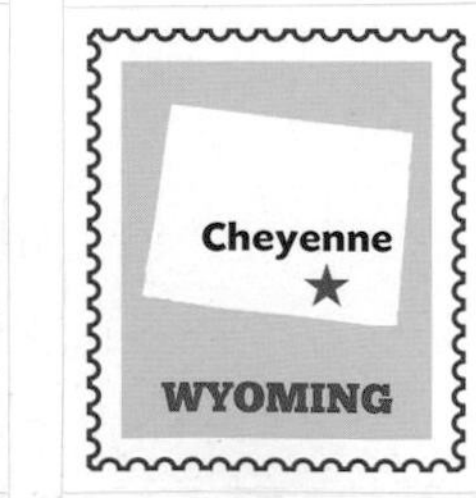

Stickers to use on page 15

Stickers to use on page 44

Stickers to use on page 63

Stickers to use on page 71

Stickers to use on page 73

Punch out these cards to create a challenging memory game of American icons. To play, lay all the cards facedown. Turn over one card and then another. If it's a match, put them to the side. If they don't match, turn them both over and try another set. Try to match all the cards in 10 turns.

Benjamin Franklin

Benjamin Franklin

The Gateway Arch

The Gateway Arch

The Golden Gate Bridge

The Golden Gate Bridge

The Empire State Building

The Empire State Building

The Liberty Bell

The Liberty Bell

The Statue of Liberty

The Statue of Liberty

Independence Hall

Independence Hall

Mount Rushmore

Mount Rushmore

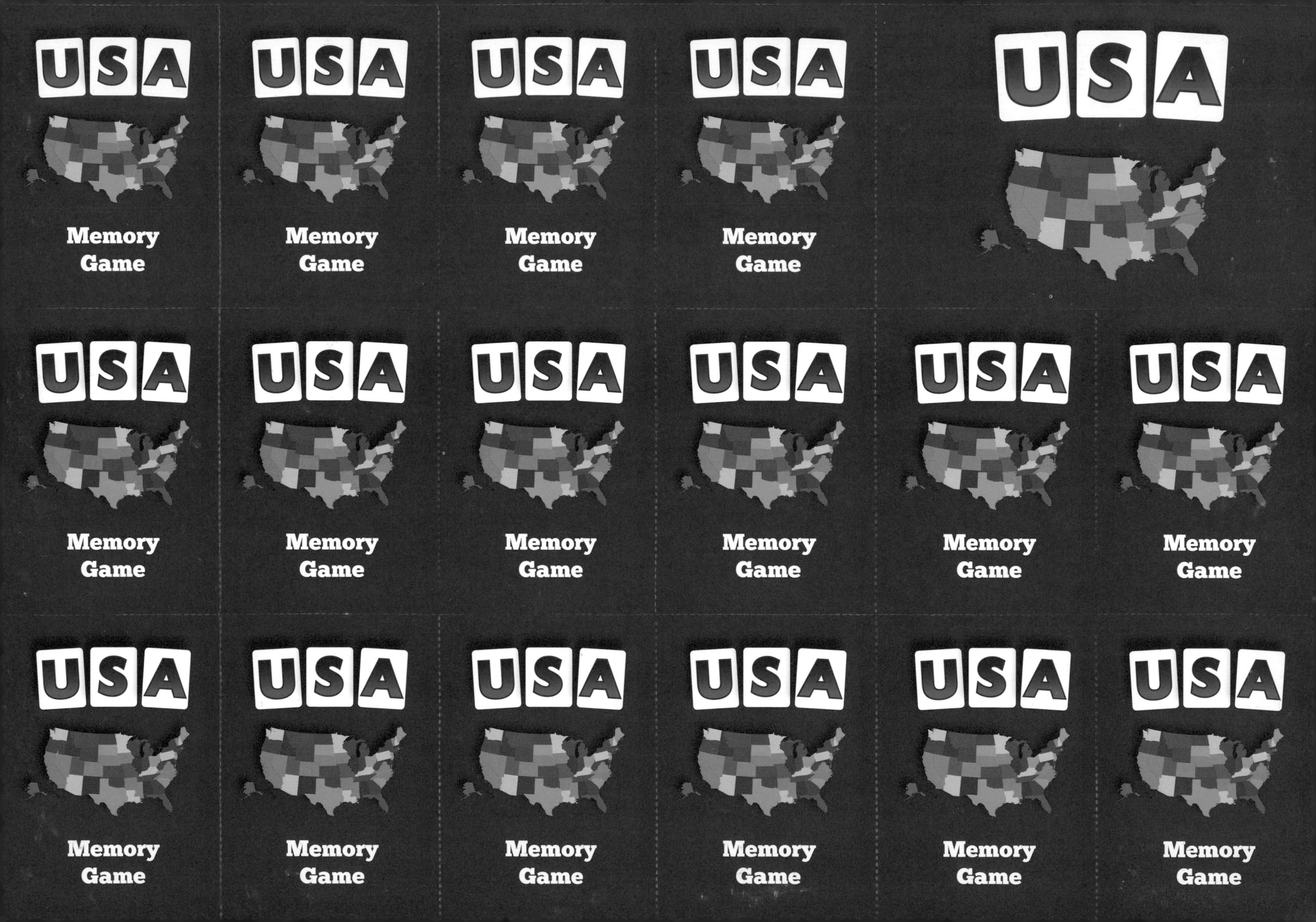

Memory Game

Memory Game

Memory Game

Memory Game

USA

USA

Memory Game

USA

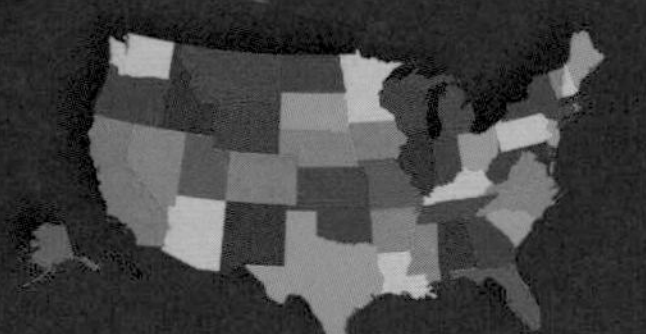

Memory Game

USA

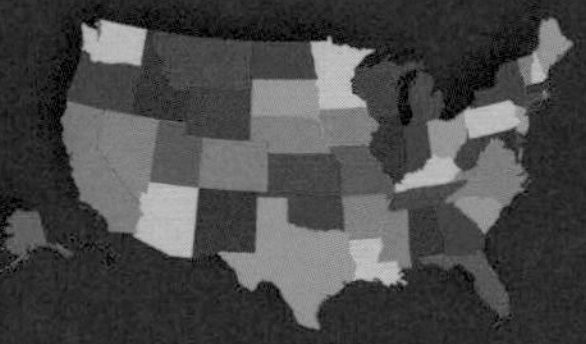

Memory Game

USA

Memory Game

USA

Memory Game

USA

Memory Game

USA

Memory Game

USA

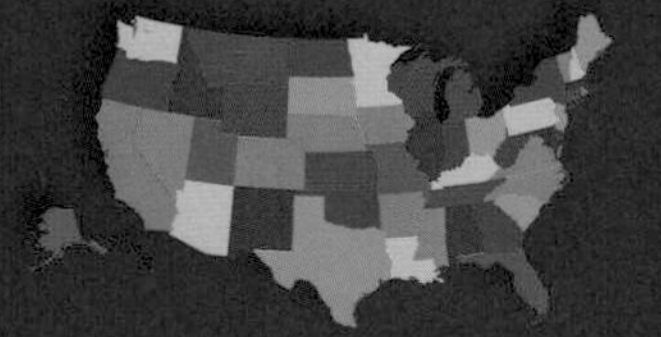

Memory Game

USA

Memory Game

USA

Memory Game

USA

Memory Game

USA

Memory Game

The Willis Tower

The Willis Tower

The Space Needle

The Space Needle

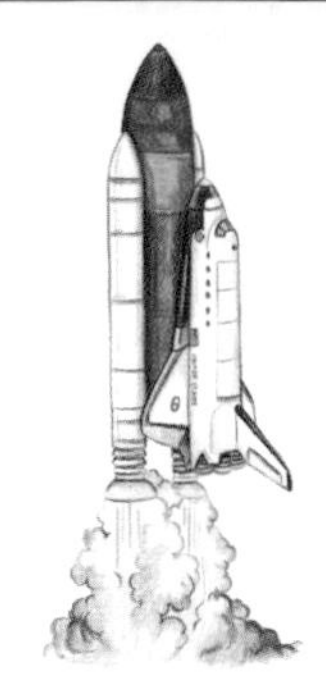

The Space Shuttle

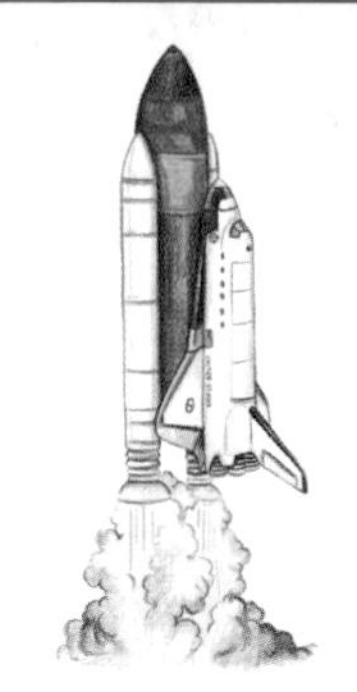

The Space Shuttle

The Alamo

The Alamo

The Mayflower

The Mayflower

Abraham Lincoln

Abraham Lincoln

George Washington

George Washington

Washington Monument

Washington Monument

The White House

The White House

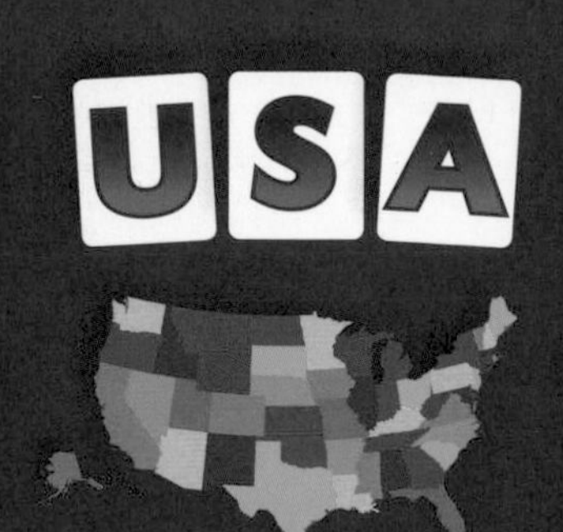

USA

Memory
Game

USA

Memory
Game

USA

Memory
Game

USA

Memory
Game

USA

Memory
Game

USA

Memory
Game

USA

Memory
Game

USA

Memory
Game

USA

Memory
Game

USA

Memory
Game

USA

Memory
Game

USA

Memory
Game

USA

Memory
Game

USA

Memory
Game

USA

Memory
Game

USA

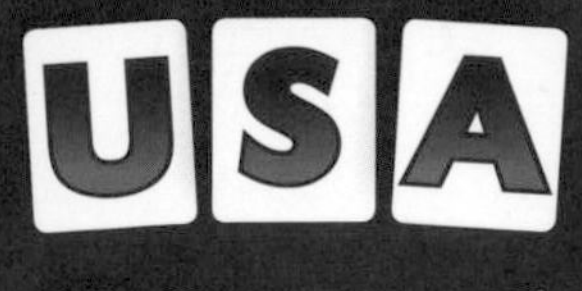

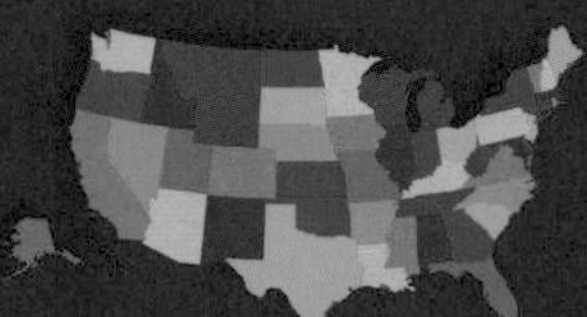

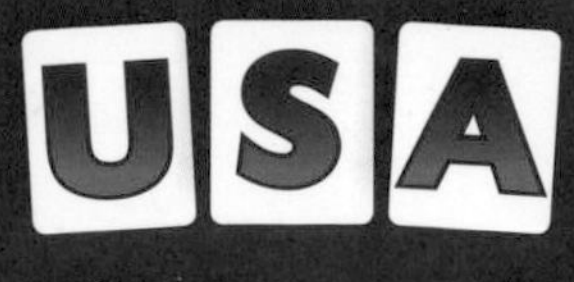

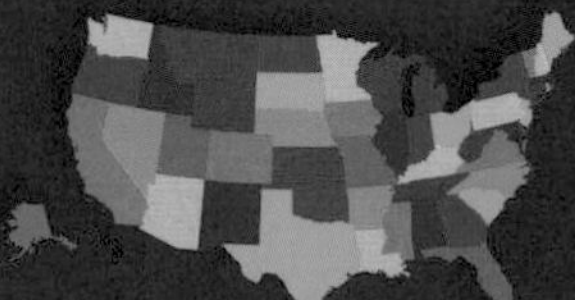

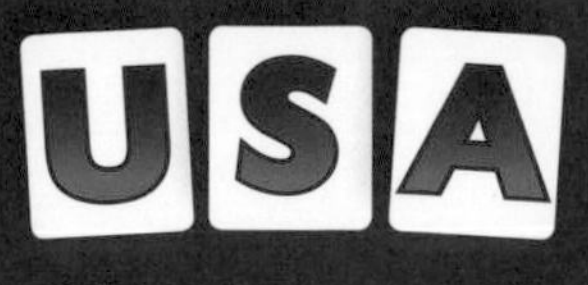

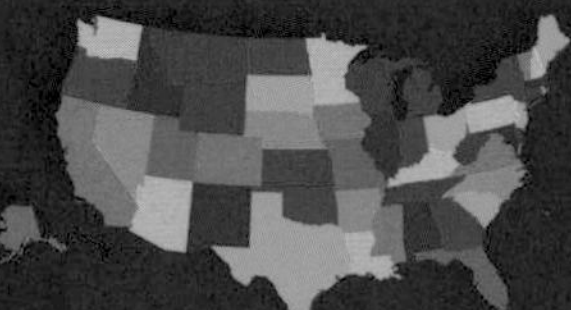

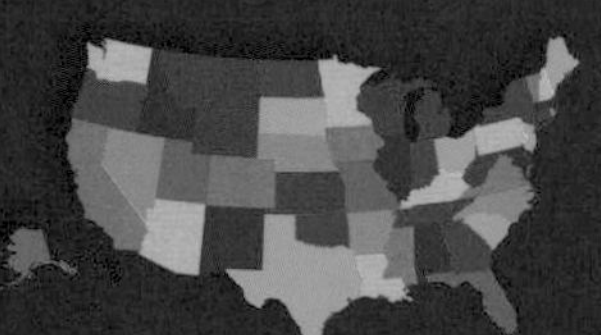

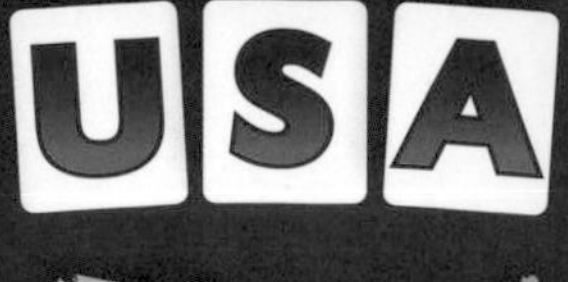

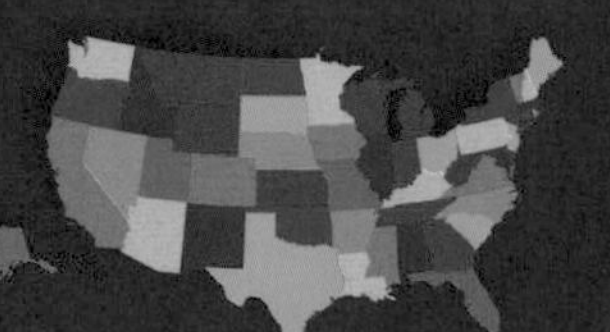

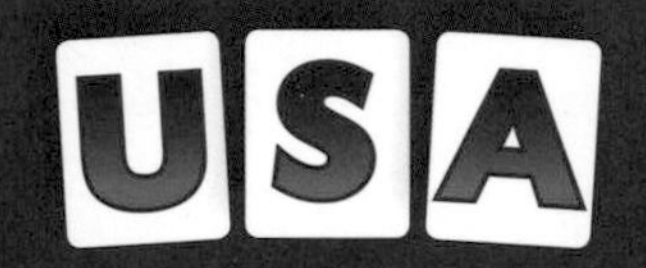

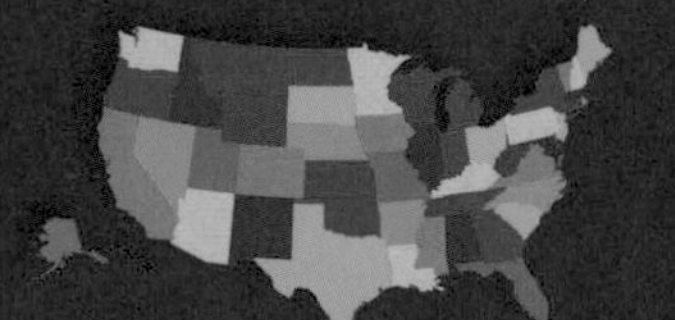

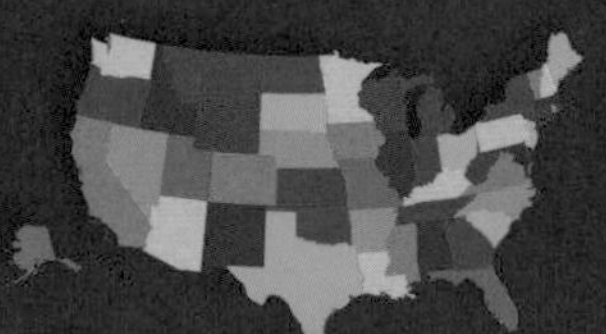

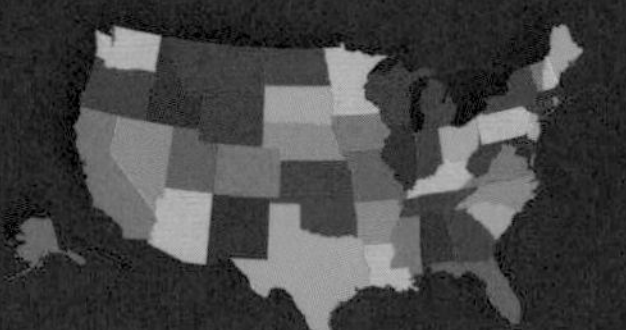

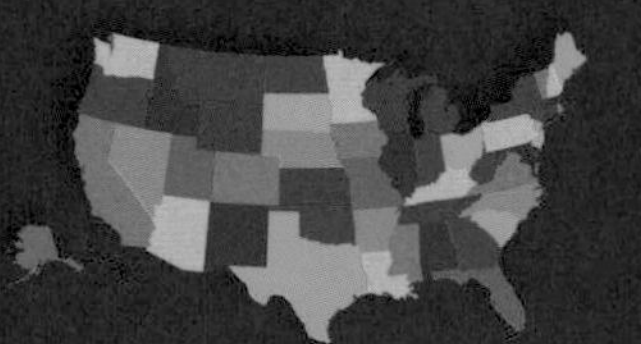

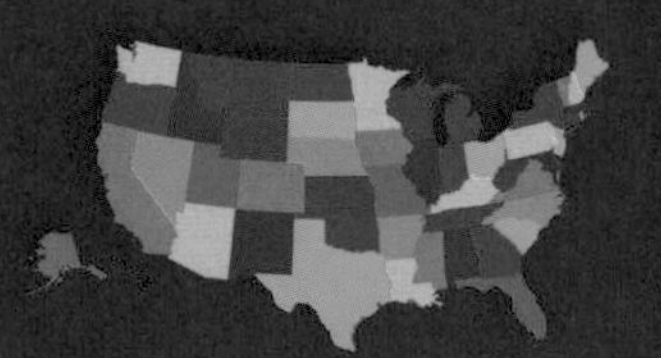

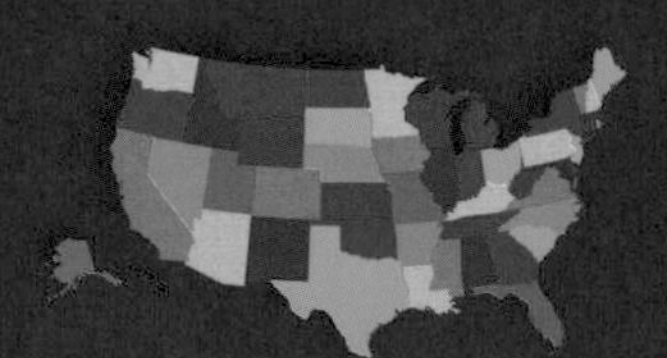

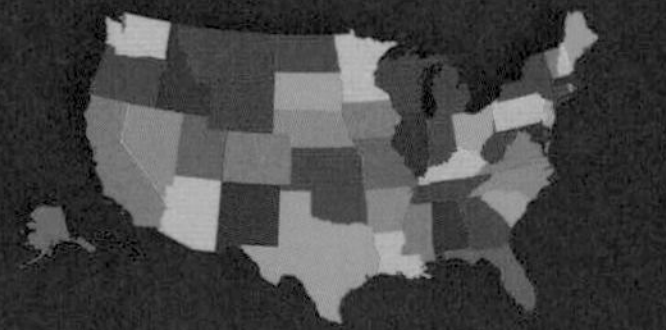

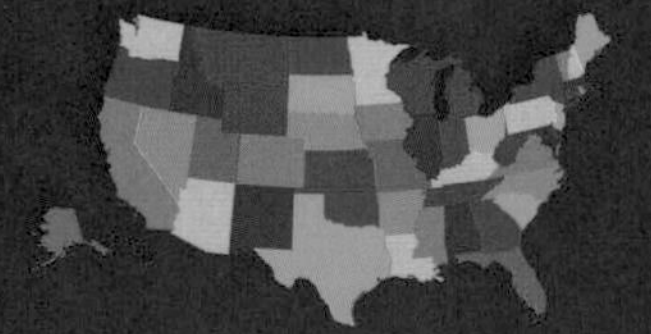

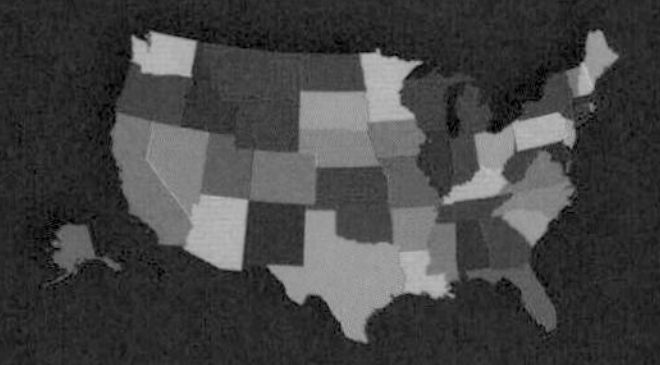

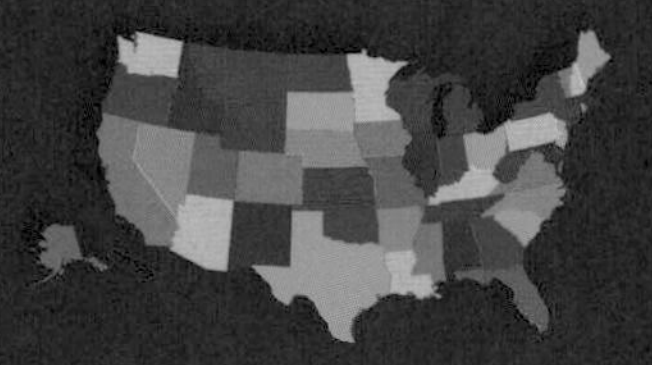

Memory
Game

USA

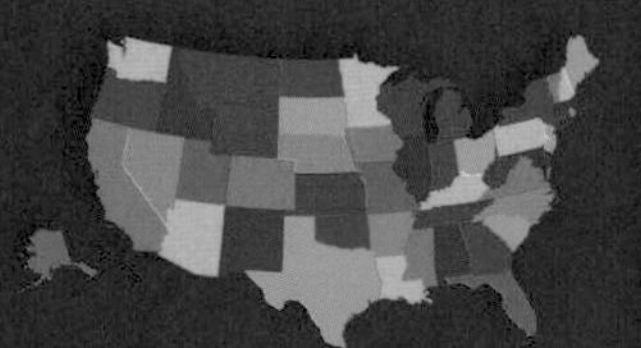

Memory
Game

USA

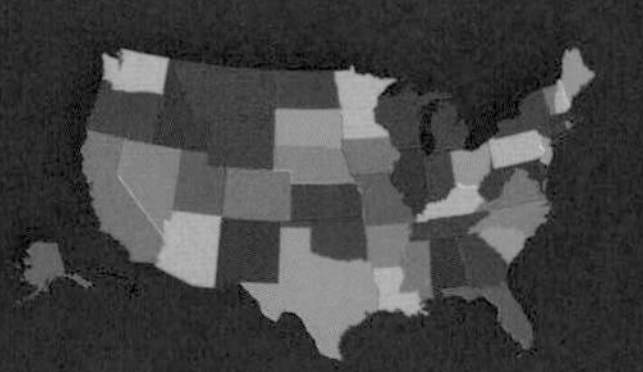

Memory
Game

Can you find all the original 13 colonies listed below? Words can be found forward, backward, and diagonally.

Pennsylvania

Georgia

Massachusetts

Virginia

Connecticut

Delaware

Maryland

New Jersey

South Carolina

New Hampshire

North Carolina

New York

Rhode Island

H	M	O	Q	V	C	N	W	M	D	G	U	S	U	A	Z	N	Q	D	N
O	I	Y	E	S	R	E	J	W	E	N	T	V	X	I	Y	O	J	Z	L
M	U	J	V	Q	K	U	R	B	P	T	W	G	K	G	I	R	J	K	R
A	Q	R	T	Z	P	E	U	A	E	X	L	S	L	R	G	T	X	H	W
R	Q	S	J	R	O	N	Q	S	W	P	S	D	G	O	U	H	N	B	Q
Y	B	K	N	O	S	O	U	K	D	A	C	Q	L	E	L	C	E	Z	A
L	I	R	R	G	F	H	G	M	I	A	L	X	J	G	B	A	W	S	I
A	L	L	T	Y	C	J	M	P	Z	C	K	E	X	X	W	R	Y	U	N
N	E	W	H	A	M	P	S	H	I	R	E	J	D	X	D	O	O	O	I
D	R	I	S	E	C	O	N	N	E	C	T	I	C	U	T	L	R	Z	G
N	C	S	S	A	I	N	A	V	L	Y	S	N	N	E	P	I	K	O	R
O	A	D	N	A	L	S	I	E	D	O	H	R	K	L	G	N	K	Q	I
M	A	N	I	L	O	R	A	C	H	T	U	O	S	G	I	A	A	M	V

Turn to page 77 for the answers.

Name the President

He was the first president of the United States.
He was born on February 22, 1732.
His wife's name was Martha.

Use the code below to fill in the blanks
and reveal the answer.

___ ___ ___ ___ ___ ___
23 24 19 9 23 24

___ ___ ___ ___ ___ ___ ___ ___ ___ ___
15 26 17 4 22 7 23 10 19 7

1=B	5=J	9=R	13=Z	17=S	21=K	25=C
2=D	6=L	10=T	14=Y	18=Q	22=I	26=A
3=F	7=N	11=V	15=W	19=O	23=G	
4=H	8=P	12=X	16=U	20=M	24=E	

Turn to page 77 for the answer.

Alabama

Find the correct sticker and place it here!

The yellowhammer
is Alabama's state bird.

Make as many words
as you can from

ALABAMA
YELLOWHAMMER

mayor

Became a State:
December 14, 1819

The 22nd State

Capital:
Montgomery

State Nickname:
Yellowhammer State,
Heart of Dixie

Fun Fact!

The black bear is the official state mammal of Alabama.

Alaska

Find the correct sticker and place it here!

See if you can find the words listed below in the word search. They can be found forward, backward, and diagonally.

Eskimo

Dogsled

X	O	O	L	G	I	J	R	I	W	I	E	N	X	K	I	E	S
E	A	J	W	F	B	C	I	Z	L	E	I	B	J	Z	H	T	D
W	X	W	S	H	E	N	P	Y	S	V	Z	R	Z	I	O	W	E
L	L	P	X	E	U	D	V	K	C	V	P	Q	G	K	X	B	L
E	I	V	E	S	R	E	I	C	A	L	G	E	E	M	E	A	S
R	L	C	S	B	T	M	A	Y	L	Z	Z	I	R	G	G	M	G
Q	M	K	O	I	O	S	B	X	W	Z	E	O	J	S	N	W	O
P	Y	Z	O	F	H	Z	N	T	N	M	S	X	Y	K	U	Q	D
O	U	P	M	X	U	N	R	S	Q	O	I	A	E	Z	M	I	F

Glacier

Igloo

Grizzly

Moose

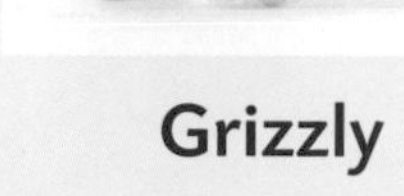

Turn to page 77 for the answers.

Became a State:
January 3, 1959

The 49th State

Capital:
Juneau

State Nickname:
The Last Frontier

Fun Fact!

Alaska is the largest state in the United States.

Arizona

Find the correct sticker and place it here!

Look at the four photos below.
One of them is different. Can you find it?

Turn to page 77 for the answer.

Became a State:
February 14, 1912

The 48th State

Capital:
Phoenix

State Nickname:
Grand Canyon State

Fun Fact!

In Arizona, you can find cactuses called saguaros, which can grow to be taller than most houses.

Arkansas

Find the correct sticker and place it here!

This type of hog is also the name of the University of Arkansas' sports teams.

Decode the letters to find out. Change each letter below to the one that comes after it in the alphabet.

Q	Z	Y	N	Q	A	Z	B	J

Turn to page 77 for the answer.

Became a State:
June 15, 1836

The 25th State

Capital:
Little Rock

State Nickname:
The Natural State

Fun Fact!

Arkansas has the only diamond field in North America.

California

Find the correct sticker and place it here!

Use the words on the right to complete this crossword puzzle.

Yosemite

Hollywood

Mount Whitney

Gold

Sacramento

Redwood

Grapes

D

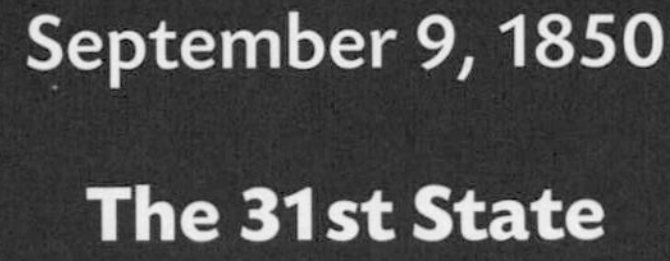

Became a State:
September 9, 1850

The 31st State

Capital:
Sacramento

State Nickname:
The Golden State

Fun Fact!

More people live in California than in any other state.

Turn to page 77 for the answers.

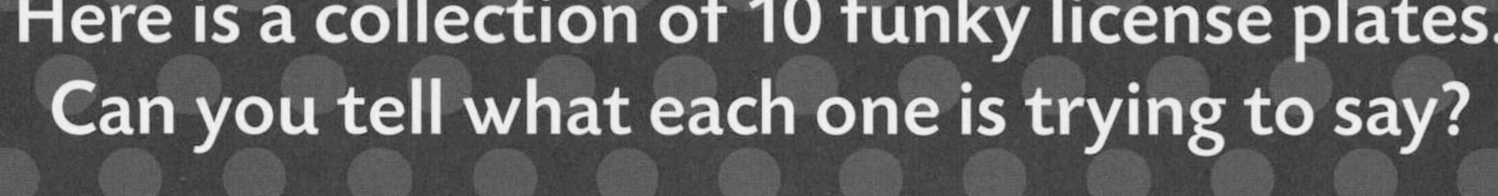

1.__________________ 2.__________________ 3.__________________ 4.__________________

5.__________________ 6.__________________ 7.__________________ 8.__________________

9.__________________ 10.__________________

Turn to page 77 for the answers.

Colorado

Find the correct sticker and place it here!

Rocky Mountain National Park is in Colorado.

Circle all the items you would take with you on a trip to the Rockies.

Became a State:
August 1, 1876

The 38th State

Capital:
Denver

State Nickname:
The Centennial State

Fun Fact!

The square dance is the official state dance of Colorado.

Connecticut

Find the
correct sticker
and place it here!

Noah Webster, who wrote the first American dictionary, was born in Connecticut.

Make as many words as you can from

DICTIONARY

can

Became a State:
January 9, 1788

The 5th State

Capital:
Hartford

State Nickname:
The Constitution State

Fun Fact!

The hamburger was invented in Connecticut!

Delaware

Find the correct sticker and place it here!

What is Delaware's state flower?

Use the code below to fill in the blanks and reveal the answer.

___ ___ ___ ___ ___
8 24 26 25 4

___ ___ ___ ___ ___ ___ ___
1 6 19 17 17 19 20

1=B	5=J	9=R	13=Z	17=S	21=K	25=C
2=D	6=L	10=T	14=Y	18=Q	22=I	26=A
3=F	7=N	11=V	15=W	19=O	23=G	
4=H	8=P	12=X	16=U	20=M	24=E	

Turn to page 77 for the answer.

Became a State:
December 7, 1787

The 1st State

Capital:
Dover

State Nickname:
The First State

Fun Fact!

The ladybug is Delaware's official state bug.

Florida

Find the
correct sticker
and place it here!

The Kennedy Space Center is located in Florida.

Cross out the word FLORIDA every time you see it. When you reach a letter that does not belong, write it in the circles below to spell the name of the launch site for the Mercury, Gemini, and Apollo space programs.

FLORIDAFLORIDACFLORIDAAFLORIDAP
FLORIDAEFLORIDAFLORIDACFLORIDA
AFLORIDAFLORIDANFLORIDAAFLORIDA
FLORIDAVFLORIDAFLORIDAEFLORIDA
FLORIDAFLORIDAFLORIDARFLORIDA
FLORIDAFLORIDAAFLORIDAFLORIDA
FLORIDAFLORIDAFLORIDALFLORIDA

Turn to page 77 for the answer.

Became a State:
March 3, 1845

The 27th State

Capital:
Tallahassee

State Nickname:
The Sunshine State

Fun Fact!

The oldest city in the United States is St. Augustine, Florida.

Welcome to the Florida Everglades!
Use the stickers in the front of the book
to create an exciting scene.

Georgia

Find the correct sticker and place it here!

Look at the four photos below.
One of them is different. Can you find it?

Turn to page 77 for the answer.

Became a State:
January 2, 1788

The 4th State

Capital:
Atlanta

State Nickname:
The Peach State

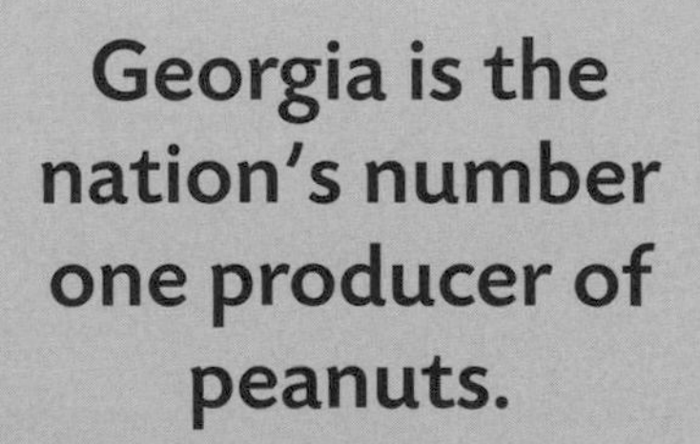

Fun Fact!

Georgia is the nation's number one producer of peanuts.

Hawaii

Find the correct sticker and place it here!

See if you can find the words listed below in the word search. They can be found forward, backward, and diagonally.

Surfer

Island

V	C	C	S	L	W	O	Z	R	Z	A	P	C	K	M	H	G	B
C	R	R	K	U	N	D	N	A	L	S	I	K	M	L	Y	F	T
H	Y	B	N	A	R	U	B	Z	E	Z	N	Y	N	Q	Y	H	G
P	N	I	C	I	F	F	X	L	M	X	E	V	D	S	R	S	A
U	J	L	Q	A	J	H	E	S	R	U	A	C	H	P	G	G	O
A	O	Y	T	R	R	L	J	R	S	Q	P	J	X	J	E	K	L
V	L	Z	J	L	U	G	M	Z	N	Z	P	G	R	H	W	V	X
D	J	X	K	K	F	H	E	R	N	A	L	U	H	Z	R	M	P
A	C	O	U	P	J	T	J	I	P	M	E	O	B	G	O	L	U

Ukulele

Volcano

Pineapple

Hula

Turn to page 77 for the answers.

Became a State:
August 21, 1959

The 50th State

Capital:
Honolulu

State Nickname:
The Aloha State

Fun Fact!

Hawaii is the only state made entirely of islands.

Challenge a friend to a game of Road Trip Bingo.
When you see something on your bingo card, mark it off.
The first person to get five in a row and shout "Bingo" wins.

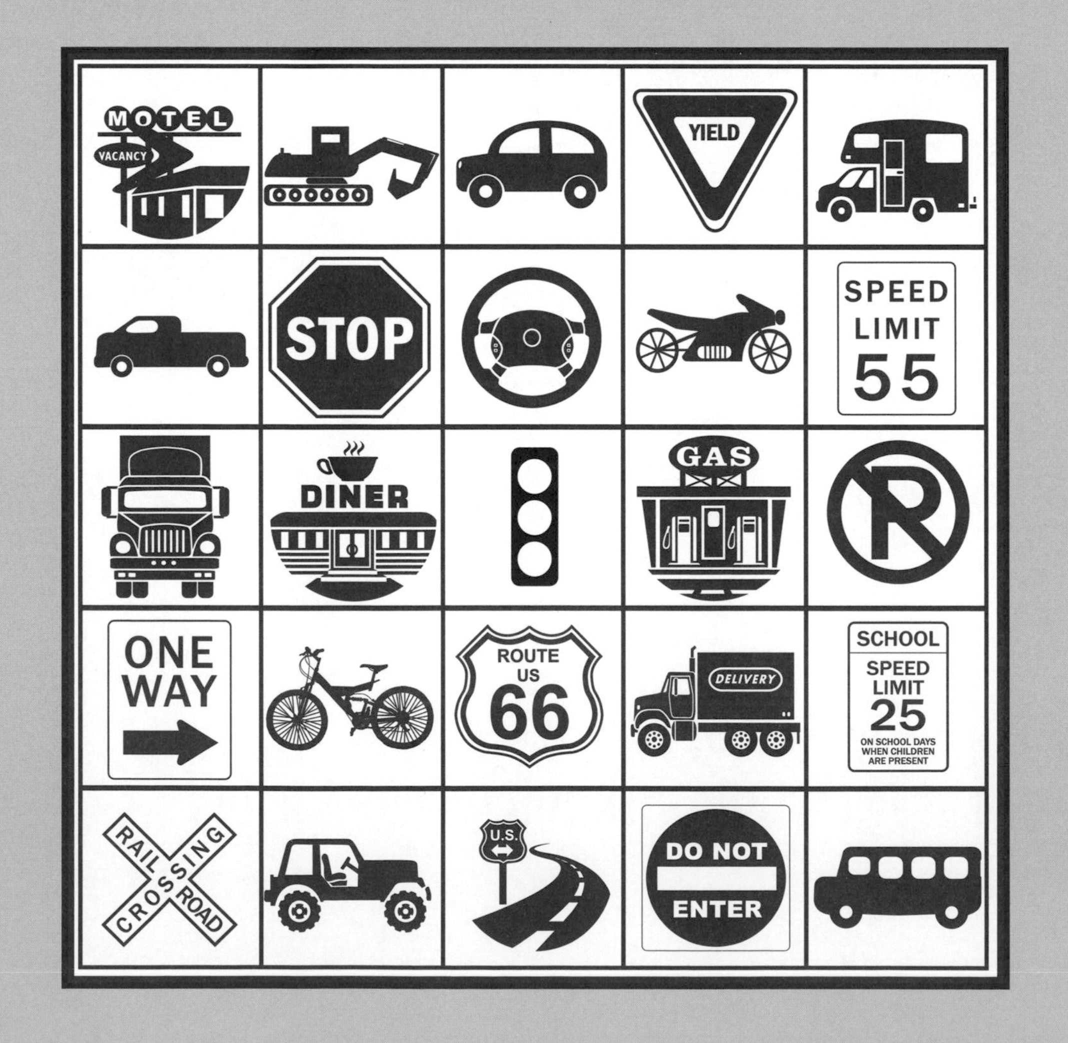

Idaho

Find the correct sticker and place it here!

Idaho is the largest producer of potatoes in the United States.

Find your way from the potato to the French fries.

Turn to page 77 for the answer.

Became a State:
July 3, 1890

The 43rd State

Capital:
Boise

State Nickname:
The Gem State

Fun Fact!

The deepest river gorge in the United States is Hell's Canyon, Idaho.

Illinois

Find the correct sticker and place it here!

Use the words on the right to complete this crossword puzzle.

Willis Tower

Chicago

Prairie State

Springfield

Jane Addams

Lincoln

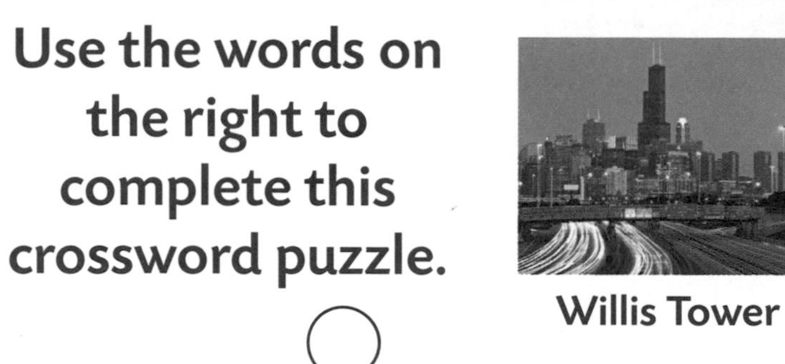

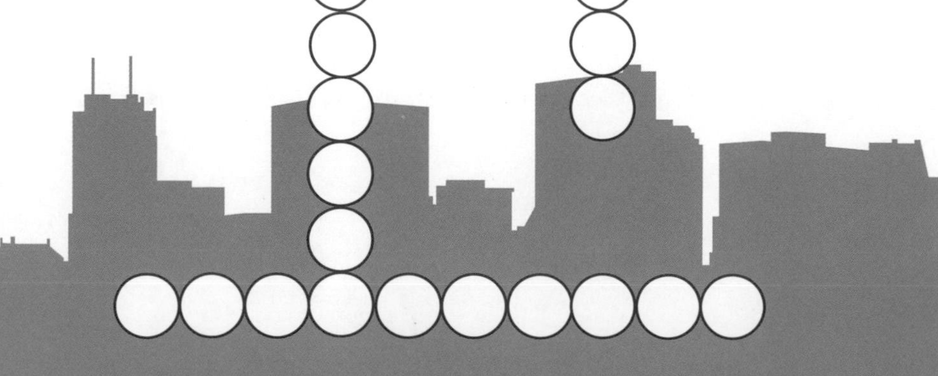

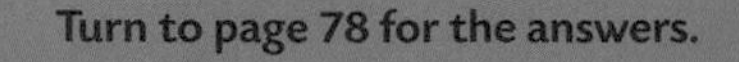

Turn to page 78 for the answers.

Became a State:
December 3, 1818

The 21st State

Capital:
Springfield

State Nickname:
The Prairie State

Fun Fact!

The world's first skyscraper was built in Chicago in 1885.

Indiana

Find the correct sticker and place it here!

Indiana is home to the Indianapolis Motor Speedway.

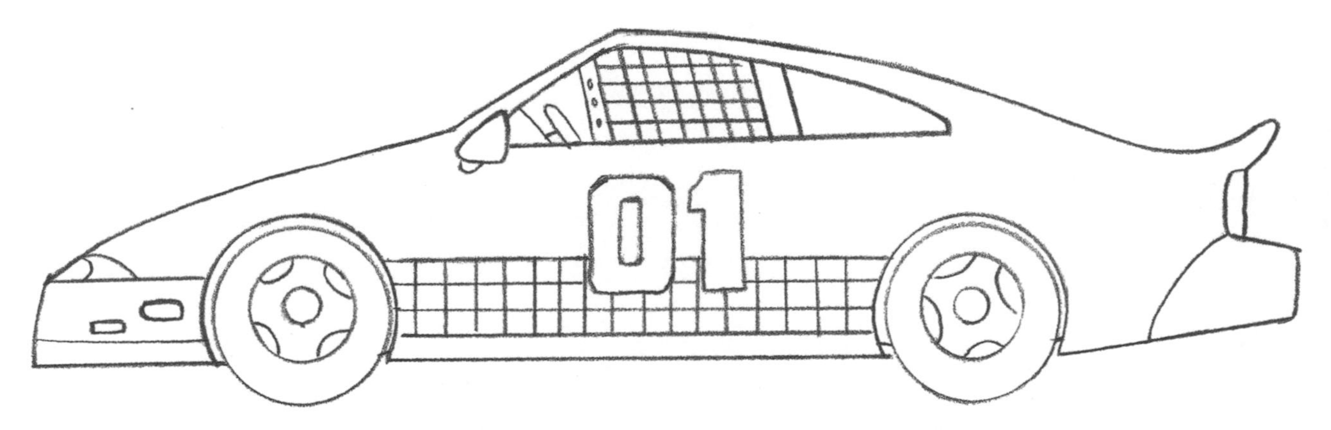

Color in the race cars.

Became a State:
December 11, 1816

The 19th State

Capital:
Indianapolis

State Nickname:
The Hoosier State

Fun Fact!

The first professional baseball game was played in Indiana.

Iowa

Find the
correct sticker
and place it here!

Did you hear the joke about the corn?
No, I didn't, but...

Decode the letters to find out the answer. Change each letter below to the one that comes before it in the alphabet.

J

B	N

B	M	M

F	B	S	T

Turn to page 78 for the answer.

Became a State:
December 28, 1846

The 29th State

Capital:
Des Moines

State Nickname:
The Hawkeye State

Fun Fact!

Iowa is called "the Food Capital of the World" because of its many farms.

Tic-tac-toe has been around for hundreds—maybe even thousands—of years. No one knows exactly when the game began, but we all know that it's just O so satisfying to get three Xs or three Os in a row (or a column or a diagonal). Go ahead, have a tic-tac-toe marathon!

Find the correct sticker and place it here!

Plenty of eye-catching sunflowers can be seen along roadsides in Kansas. Look at the four photos below. One of them is different. Can you find it?

Turn to page 78 for the answer.

Became a State:
January 29, 1861

The 34th State

Capital:
Topeka

State Nickname:
The Sunflower State

Fun Fact!

The graham cracker was invented in Kansas.

Kentucky

Find the correct sticker and place it here!

The famous Kentucky Derby horse race is held in Louisville, Kentucky.

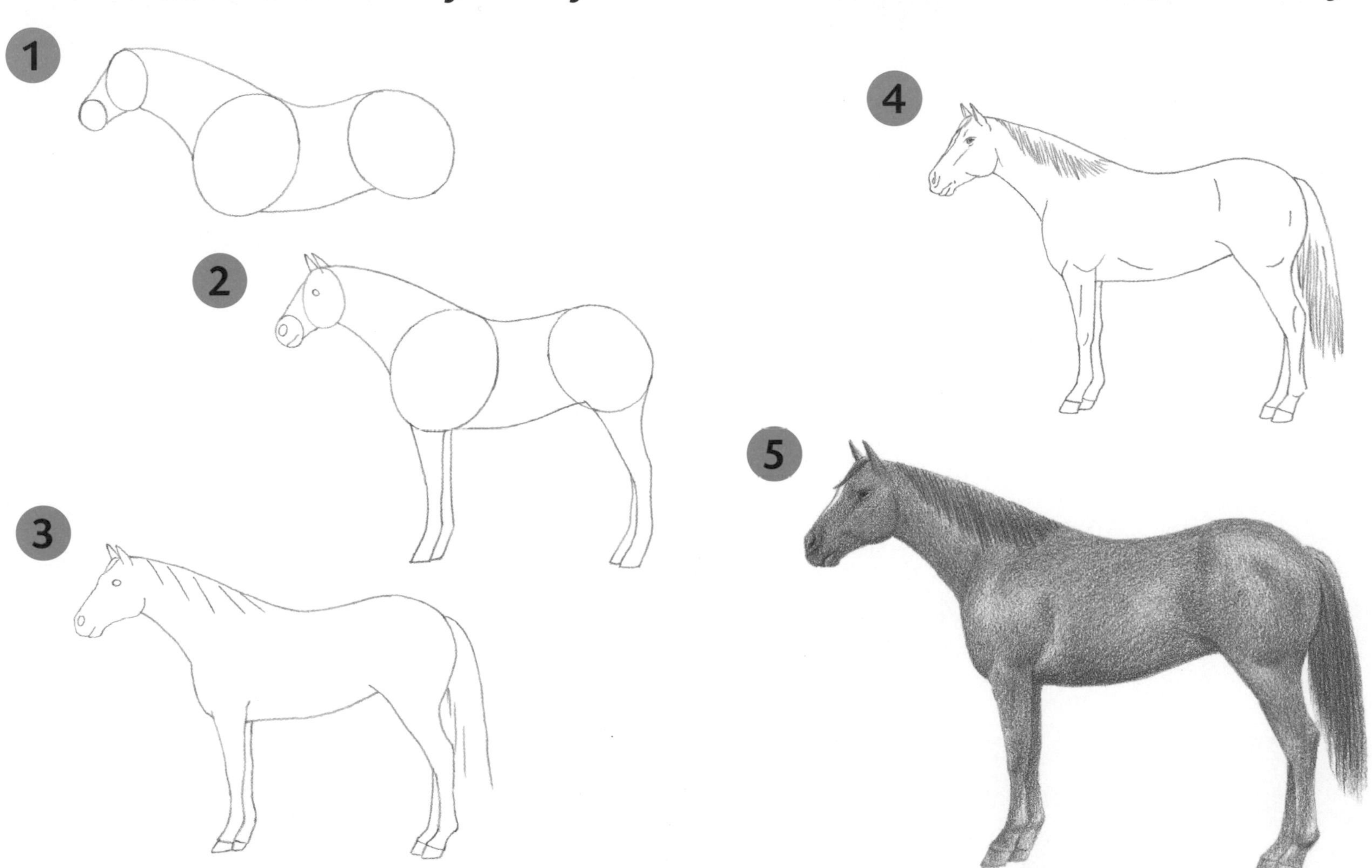

Follow the steps above to draw a horse.

Became a State:
June 1, 1792

The 15th State

Capital:
Frankfort

State Nickname:
The Bluegrass State

Fun Fact!

The largest amount of gold stored anywhere in the world is at Fort Knox in Kentucky.

Name the President

He was the 16th president.
He was president during the Civil War.
His home state was Illinois.

Use the code below to fill in the blanks
and reveal the answer.

___	___	___	___	___	___	___
26	1	9	26	4	26	20

___	___	___	___	___	___	___
6	22	7	25	19	6	7

1=B	5=J	9=R	13=Z	17=S	21=K	25=C
2=D	6=L	10=T	14=Y	18=Q	22=I	26=A
3=F	7=N	11=V	15=W	19=O	23=G	
4=H	8=P	12=X	16=U	20=M	24=E	

Turn to page 78 for the answer.

Louisana

Find the correct sticker and place it here!

See if you can find the words listed below in the word search. They can be found forward, backward, and diagonally.

Alligator

Bayou

R	K	C	C	X	L	P	U	U	G	U	C	T	E	N	Z	N	I	N	Q
B	H	N	J	E	C	H	J	Y	F	N	O	H	C	D	U	E	I	B	M
U	A	R	Y	H	U	G	D	P	W	S	N	Y	V	Q	Q	W	O	A	P
B	R	T	A	C	C	B	V	F	J	B	R	B	A	K	P	O	P	F	X
L	Q	C	T	L	S	A	R	G	I	D	R	A	M	B	E	R	Y	W	R
Y	G	T	F	Y	L	V	C	B	A	A	O	N	S	S	L	L	G	J	H
J	R	I	C	C	H	I	G	I	B	Y	B	I	V	Y	I	E	U	A	B
G	I	K	S	W	V	B	G	Z	F	F	Y	F	A	B	C	A	D	Z	J
P	K	L	F	Y	X	P	U	A	Z	E	I	Y	I	P	A	N	K	Z	F
D	O	K	I	W	A	N	C	X	T	D	Y	R	N	G	N	S	U	R	U
T	D	W	O	K	G	Q	S	N	V	O	V	B	K	P	S	E	V	O	A
A	U	T	O	K	X	V	N	A	M	V	R	Y	S	S	P	S	W	B	O

Pelican

Jazz

Mardi Gras

New Orleans

Turn to page 78 for the answers.

Became a State:
April 30, 1812

The 18th State

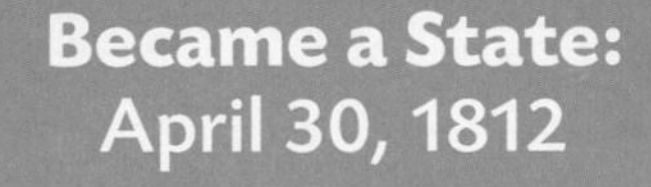

Capital:
Baton Rouge

State Nickname:
The Pelican State

Fun Fact!

The American alligator is Louisiana's state reptile.

Maine

Find the correct sticker and place it here!

Maine is known for being one of the largest producers of lobster in the United States.

One of these lobsters is different from the others. Circle it.

Turn to page 78 for the answer.

Became a State:
March 15, 1820

The 23rd State

Capital:
Augusta

State Nickname:
The Pine Tree State

Fun Fact!

Maine has over 3,000 islands.

When you take a road trip, it's always best to allow extra time for getting lost! Find your way home in this highway maze.

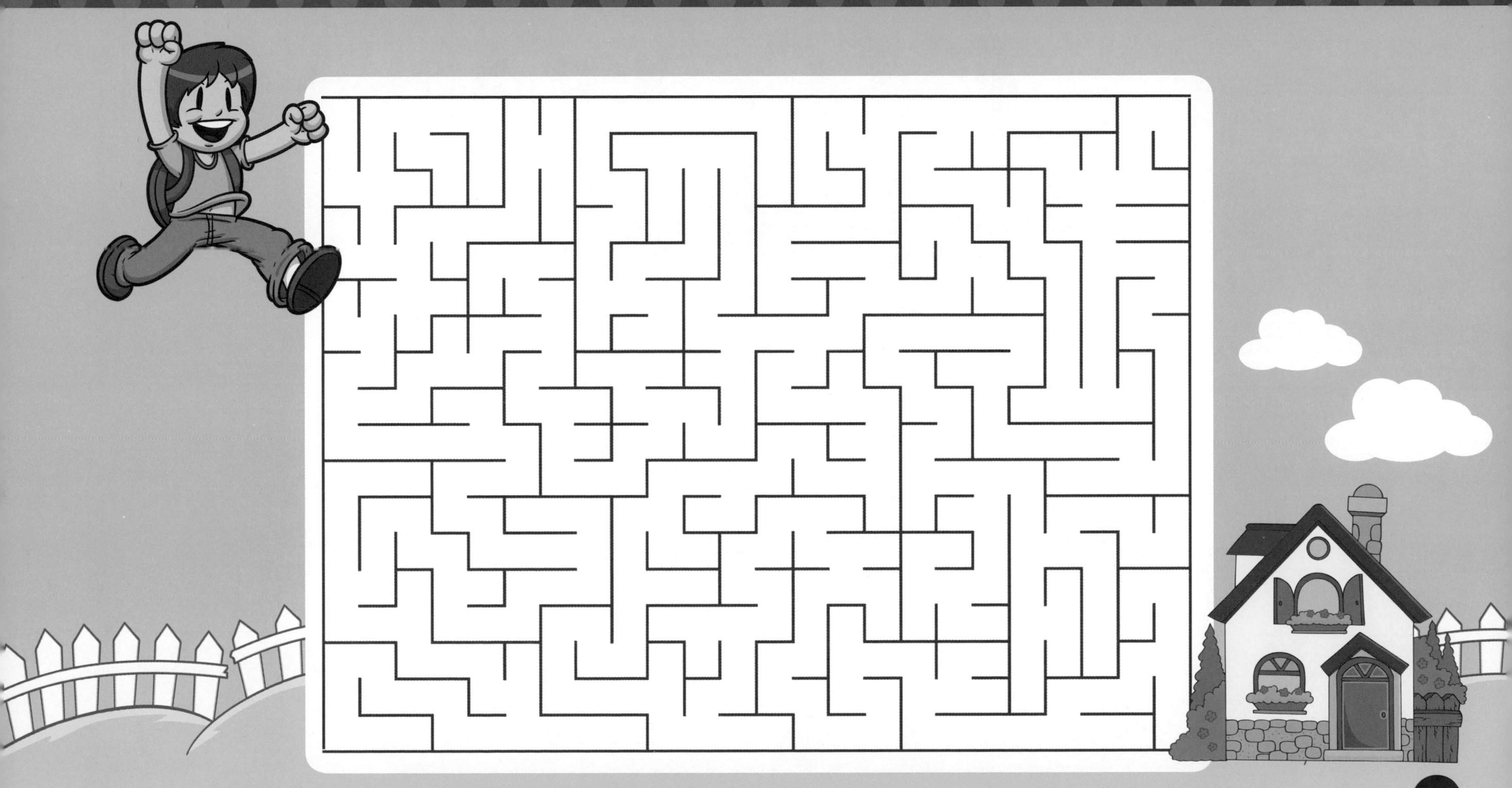

Turn to page 78 for the answer.

Maryland

Find the correct sticker and place it here!

Annapolis

MARYLAND

What's the name of Maryland's state bird as well as Baltimore's baseball team?

Decode the letters to find out. Change each letter below to the one that comes after it in the alphabet.

N	Q	H	N	K	D	R

Turn to page 78 for the answer.

Became a State:
April 28, 1788

The 7th State

Capital:
Annapolis

State Nickname:
The Old Line State

Fun Fact!

Jousting is Maryland's official state sport.

Massachusetts

Find the correct sticker and place it here!

April showers brings May flowers, but what do *Mayflowers* bring?

Cross out the word MASSACHUSETTS every time you see it. When you reach a letter that does not belong, write it in the circles below to spell the secret word.

MASSACHUSETTSPMASSACHUSETTS
IMASSACHUSETTSLMASSACHUSETTS
MASSACHUSETTSGMASSACHUSETTSR
MASSACHUSETTSMASSACHUSETTSI
MASSACHUSETTSMMASSACHUSETTS
SMASSACHUSETTSMASSACHUSETTS

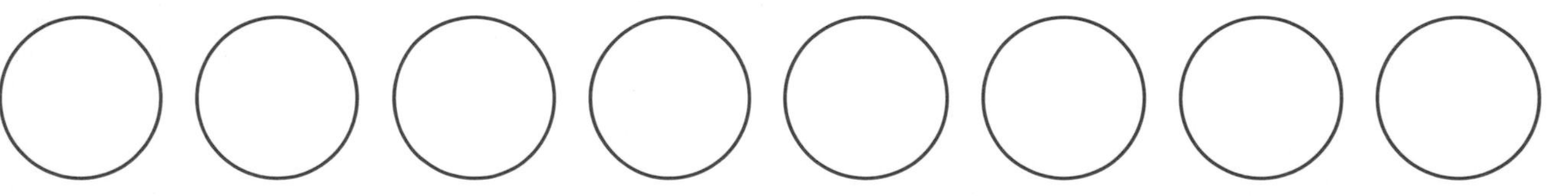

Turn to page 78 for the answer.

Became a State:
February 6, 1788

The 6th State

Capital:
Boston

State Nickname:
The Bay State

Fun Fact!

America's first public school was founded in Boston, Massachusetts, in 1635.

Michigan

Find the correct sticker and place it here!

Unscramble the words to reveal the names of the Great Lakes.

ORPRUESI [S] ___ [P] ___ ___ ___ ___ ___

HMIACING [M] ___ ___ ___ ___ [G] ___ ___

ARNOTOI [O] ___ [T] ___ ___ ___ [O]

NUROH [H] ___ ___ ___ [N]

IRRE [E] ___ ___ [E]

Turn to page 78 for the answers.

Became a State:
January 26, 1837

The 26th State

Capital:
Lansing

State Nickname:
The Great Lakes State

Fun Fact!

Michigan has more lighthouses (150) than any other state.

Minnesota

Find the correct sticker and place it here!

Circle the items that you would take with you for a day at the lake.

Became a State:
May 11, 1858

The 32nd State

Capital:
Saint Paul

State Nickname:
The North Star State

Fun Fact!

Milk is the official state drink of Minnesota.

Mississippi

Find the
correct sticker
and place it here!

Help the steamship return to the docks.

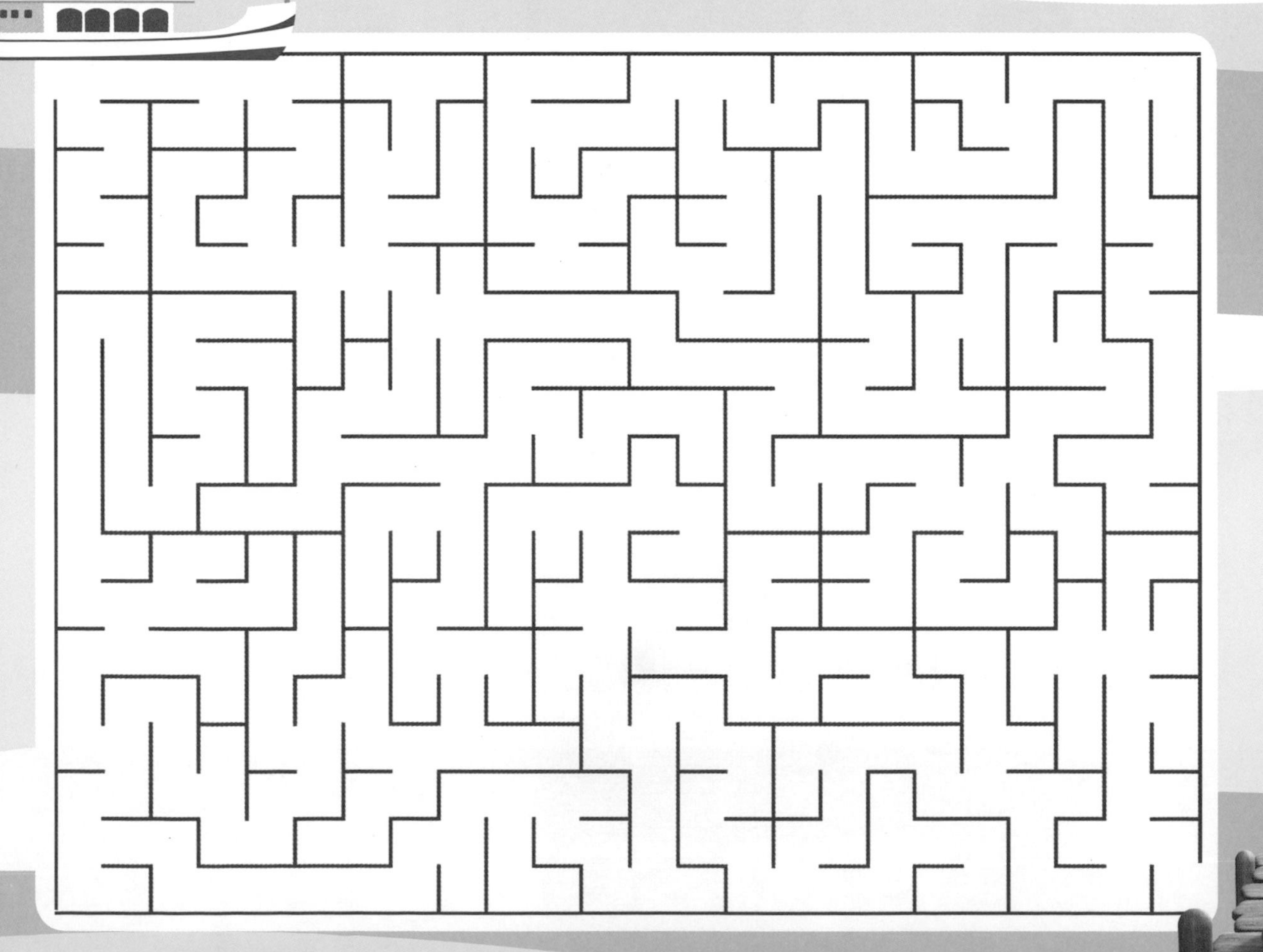

Turn to page 78 for the answer.

Became a State:
December 10, 1817

The 20th State

Capital:
Jackson

State Nickname:
The Magnolia
State

Fun Fact!

Root beer was invented in Mississippi in 1898.

Missouri

Find the correct sticker and place it here!

What is this famous structure called?

Decode the letters to find out. Change each letter below to the one that comes before it in the alphabet.

H	B	U	F	X	B	Z

B	S	D	I

Turn to page 78 for the answer.

Became a State:
August 10, 1821

The 24th State

Capital:
Jefferson City

State Nickname:
The Show Me State

Fun Fact!

The first ice-cream cone was sold at the 1904 World's Fair in St. Louis, Missouri.

American Symbols

Use the words at right to complete this crossword puzzle.

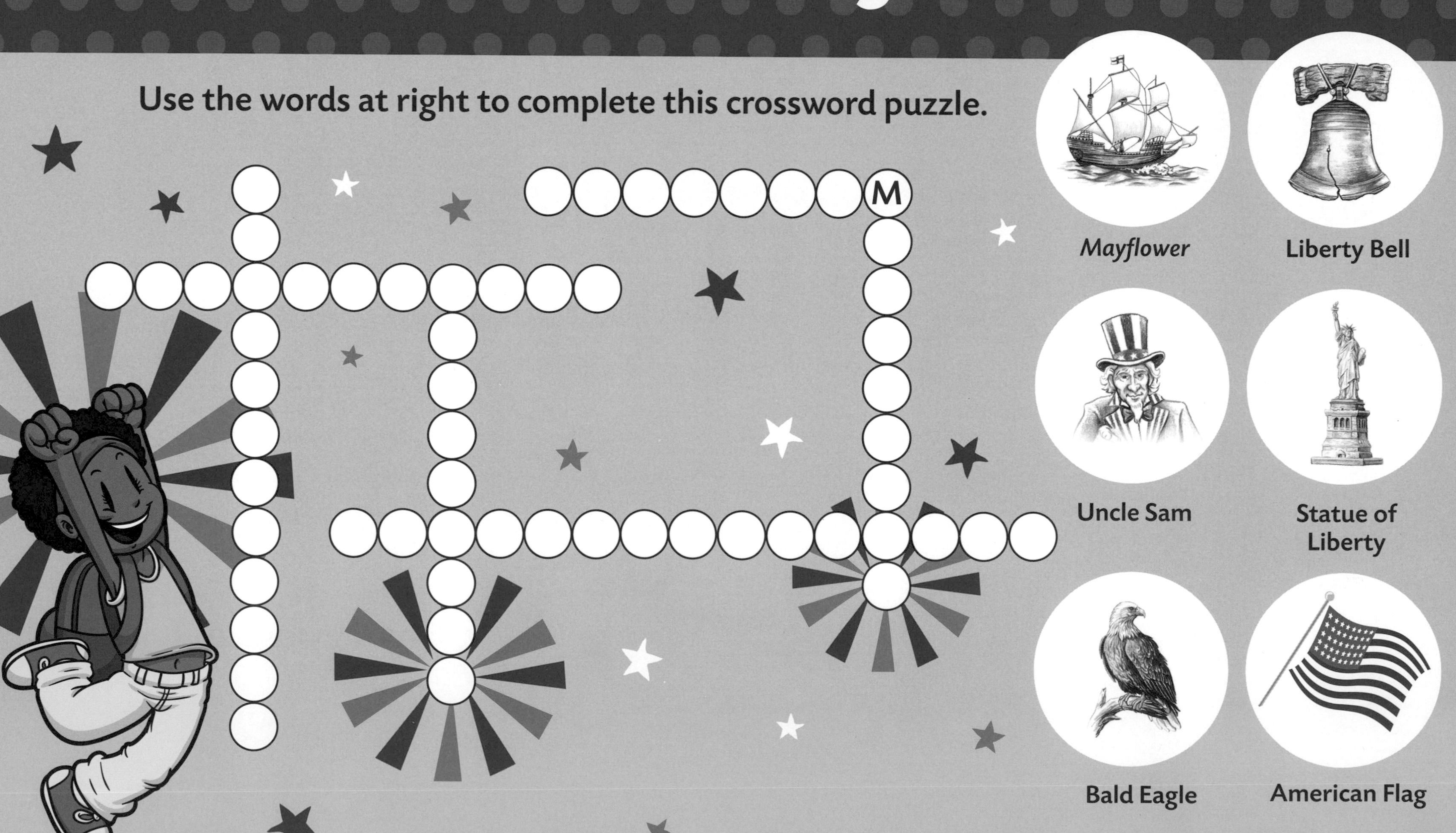

Turn to page 78 for the answers.

Montana

Find the correct sticker and place it here!

What famous Native American chief led his people in the Battle of the Little Bighorn?

Use the code below to fill in the blanks and reveal the answer.

___	___	___	___	___
25	9	26	13	14

___	___	___	___	___
4	19	9	17	24

1=B	8=P	15=W	22=I
2=D	9=R	16=U	23=G
3=F	10=T	17=S	24=E
4=H	11=V	18=Q	25=C
5=J	12=X	19=O	26=A
6=L	13=Z	20=M	
7=N	14=Y	21=K	

Turn to page 79 for the answer.

Became a State:
November 8, 1889

The 41st State

Capital:
Helena

State Nickname:
The Treasure State

Fun Fact!

In Montana, there are more elk, deer, and antelope than humans.

Nebraska

Find the correct sticker and place it here!

Lincoln

NEBRASKA

During the 1830s and 1840s, many pioneers settled in Nebraska.

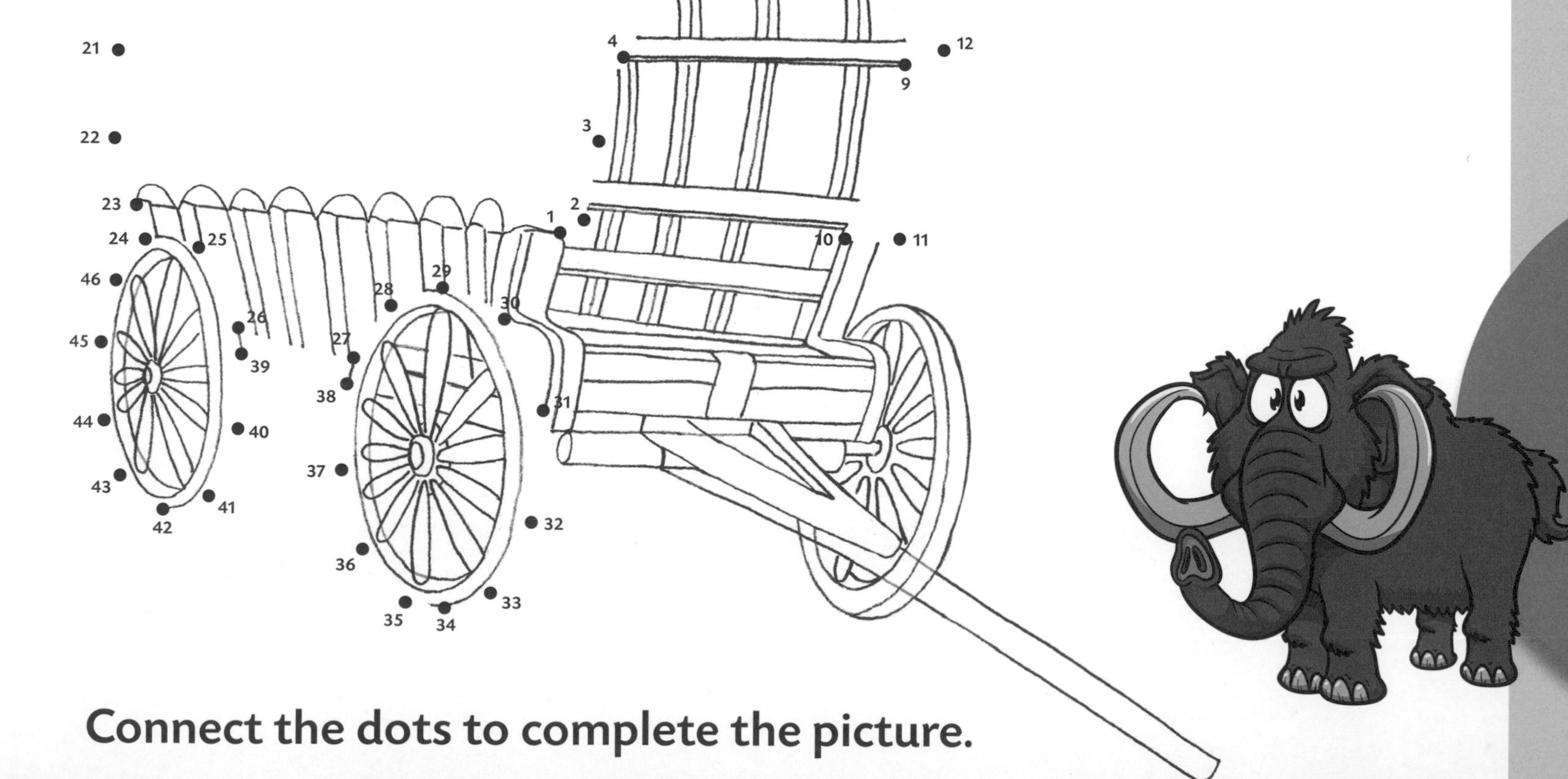

Connect the dots to complete the picture.

Became a State:
March 1, 1867

The 37th State

Capital:
Lincoln

State Nickname:
The Cornhusker State

Fun Fact!

The mammoth is the official state fossil of Nebraska.

To show your Fourth of July spirit, find all the words in the list below. They can be found forward, backward, and diagonally.

Fireworks

Independence

Flag

Barbecue

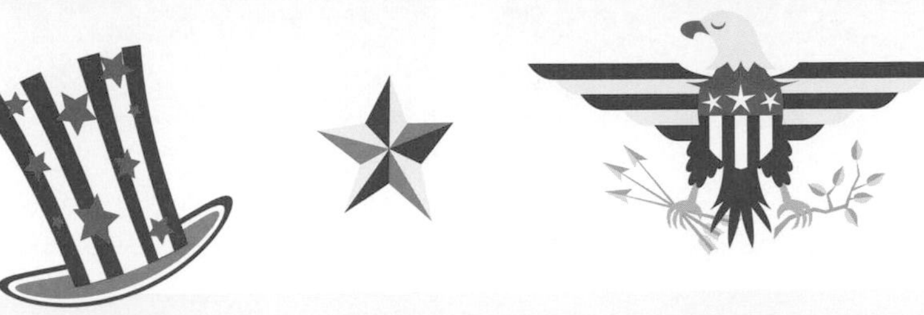

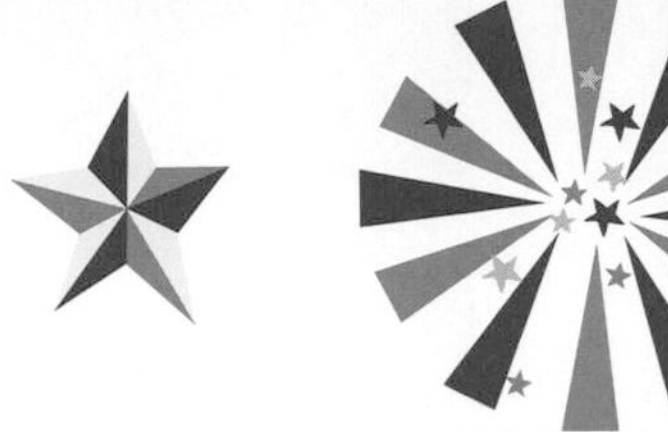

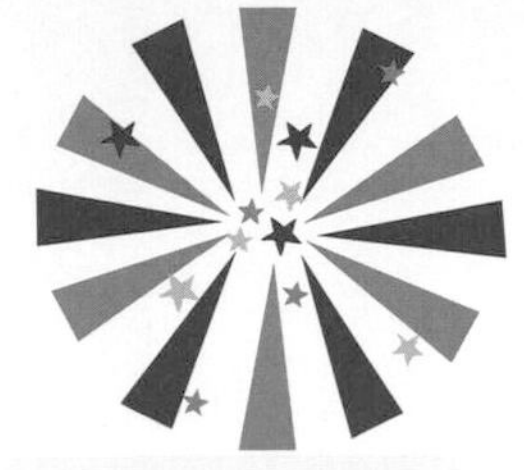

E	L	C	I	S	P	O	P	Z	M	O	G	K	E	V	S	N	S	R	M
C	M	M	P	A	N	U	R	E	G	R	U	B	M	A	H	Z	H	V	S
N	Y	F	A	S	R	L	O	W	Q	Z	I	Z	Q	I	D	I	M	C	I
E	M	I	A	W	H	V	B	O	D	R	M	F	P	X	Q	V	C	V	T
D	N	V	I	Z	F	V	N	U	T	P	X	V	L	F	E	L	A	B	O
N	C	C	V	L	W	F	Z	R	Z	A	R	C	K	A	H	E	B	A	I
E	K	B	L	K	M	T	R	G	B	K	M	L	Y	F	G	M	Y	R	R
P	Y	U	B	Z	L	S	K	R	O	W	E	R	I	F	N	O	G	B	T
E	X	D	M	X	N	V	D	S	R	S	A	U	J	A	Q	N	J	E	A
D	R	U	E	C	H	P	G	G	O	A	C	Y	T	R	R	A	J	C	P
N	D	J	X	J	E	K	L	N	L	Z	J	L	C	G	M	D	N	U	I
I	R	H	W	V	X	D	J	X	K	U	F	H	E	R	N	E	T	E	M

Turn to page 79 for the answers.

Patriotism

Popsicle

Lemonade

Hamburger

Nevada

Find the correct sticker and place it here!

Carson City

NEVADA

Hoover Dam is located near Boulder City, Nevada. It's 726 feet tall. Look at the four photos below. One of them is different. Can you find it?

Turn to page 79 for the answer.

Became a State:
October 31, 1864

The 36th State

Capital:
Carson City

State Nickname:
The Silver State

Fun Fact!

Nevada produces 80 percent of all the gold mined in the United States.

New Hampshire

Find the correct sticker and place it here!

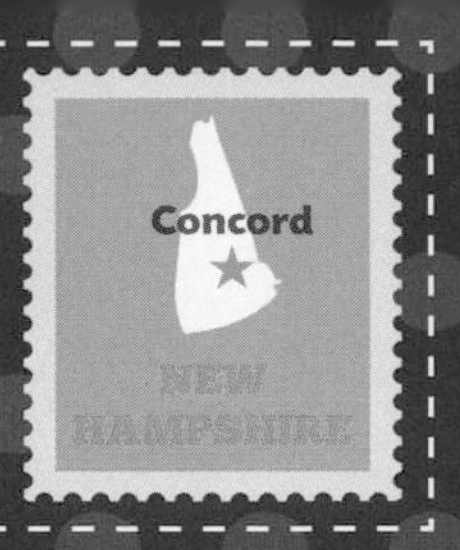

New Hampshire's state bird is the purple finch.

Make as many words as you can from

PURPLE FINCH

chirp

Became a State:
June 21, 1788

The 9th State

Capital:
Concord

State Nickname:
The Granite State

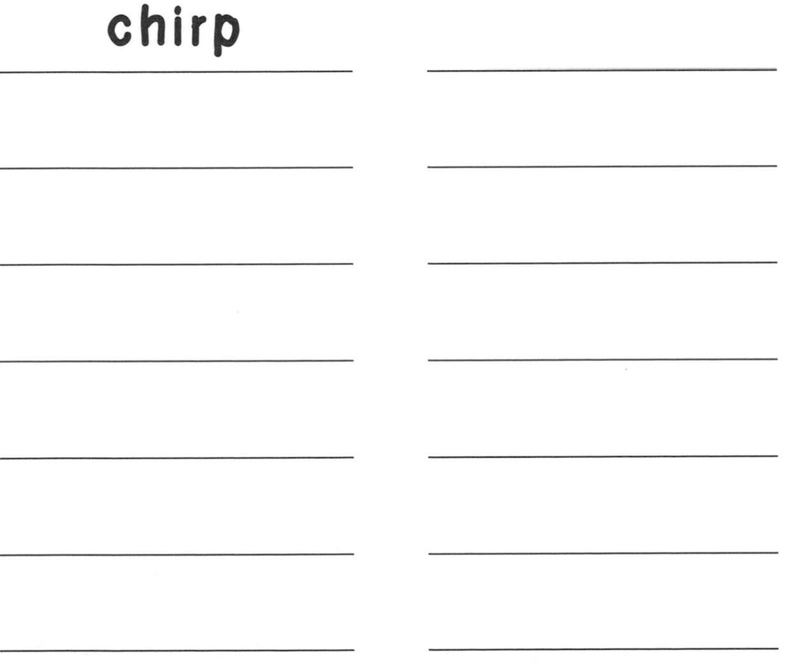

Fun Fact!

The first public library in the world was founded in 1833 in New Hampshire.

Can you find the American heroes listed below in this word search? They can be found forward, backward, and diagonally.

Benjamin Franklin

Betsy Ross

Harriet Tubman

Paul Revere

B E O F B J V E S A T N O H A C O P P Z C V
C Q J N H N I L K N A R F N I M A J N E B G
Q C W R A U B P P G W K S F Z P B E Y B B D
B N X Z R L E Z V G T S U D P P V L U P D T
I F Z L R I N C N Z O H H T R O R Y A H D I
M K Y A I F B U K R L K Z Z J I M T U P O C
F B S D E F B G Y R Z E R E V E R L U A P S
P F T H T W D S W J C I A B I I F X D K M K
S P H B T L T B N H G O D K C T K G B B D W
W R S A U E G R W G F S L K K Y L C W I V W
V W K A B X C G A P K F H V V P A Z V T Z N
T A Q F M L V R T V C E F K D U B D F V K I
T Q Y B A R G C A E N I C F F U T L U E Z K
A R W B N B E A I R I K P J C X Z B J T Y G
J U S A D U M Q Y M N X W S X D G V W L H J
S N I J A S S A L G U O D K C I R E D E R F
E E I L H Z P H J A N E A D D A M S M N Y Z

Turn to page 79 for the answers.

Jane Addams

Frederick Douglass

Patrick Henry

Pocahontas

New Jersey

Find the correct sticker and place it here!

What famous American victory began with George Washington crossing the Delaware River into New Jersey?

___ ___ ___   ___ ___ ___ ___ ___ ___
10 4 24   1 26 10 10 6 24

___ ___   ___ ___ ___ ___ ___ ___ ___
19 3   10 9 24 7 10 19 7

1=B	8=P	15=W	22=I
2=D	9=R	16=U	23=G
3=F	10=T	17=S	24=E
4=H	11=V	18=Q	25=C
5=J	12=X	19=O	26=A
6=L	13=Z	20=M	
7=N	14=Y	21=K	

Turn to page 79 for the answer.

Became a State:
December 18, 1787

The 3rd State

Capital:
Trenton

State Nickname:
The Garden State

Fun Fact!

The longest boardwalk in the world is in Atlantic City, New Jersey.

Welcome to the open highway!
Use the stickers in the front of the book
to create a fun adventure scene.

New Mexico

Find the correct sticker and place it here!

The International Balloon Fiesta takes place in Albuquerque, New Mexico.

Color in this hot-air balloon.

Became a State:
January 6, 1912

The 47th State

Capital:
Santa Fe

State Nickname:
The Land of Enchantment

Fun Fact!

There are more sheep and cattle in New Mexico than there are people.

New York

Find the correct sticker and place it here!

See if you can find the words listed below in the word search. They can be found forward, backward, and diagonally.

Statue of Liberty

Niagara Falls

Broadway

Adirondacks

Empire State

Apples

V	M	W	V	Q	G	N	V	L	G	M	S	M	J	H	C	H	L	P	Y	I	G	K
F	N	A	Q	M	A	Z	D	Y	F	H	D	F	T	N	R	M	T	P	X	S	B	V
Y	S	C	A	S	T	A	T	U	E	O	F	L	I	B	E	R	T	Y	B	E	H	E
O	E	E	N	W	Y	B	U	H	Z	D	Q	D	A	J	Y	X	P	T	N	J	H	G
R	N	H	L	T	J	L	H	U	N	B	S	A	D	P	B	O	J	F	Q	V	A	B
R	X	X	V	P	J	U	C	I	H	B	G	T	I	R	E	B	X	D	K	I	T	B
N	E	A	E	Z	P	B	P	Y	C	G	V	Y	R	U	F	X	D	U	Q	M	R	I
N	I	A	G	A	R	A	F	A	L	L	S	W	O	B	D	J	I	B	F	O	Z	B
X	O	G	Z	Q	D	B	O	J	O	V	K	C	N	T	T	S	Z	T	A	R	P	O
D	C	V	W	Q	T	C	E	U	R	C	V	Y	D	A	M	Z	G	D	M	H	X	A
B	C	G	O	I	Q	H	M	N	Q	Y	D	U	A	T	U	P	W	H	P	N	L	S
R	S	T	I	K	R	E	I	J	F	U	N	P	C	E	L	A	W	K	H	Z	K	B
F	S	V	T	G	C	S	H	L	H	B	O	H	K	S	Y	H	H	C	T	H	T	D
T	Y	Q	E	A	C	V	K	I	E	T	A	T	S	E	R	I	P	M	E	R	V	C

Turn to page 79 for the answers.

Became a State:
July 26, 1788

The 11th State

Capital:
Albany

State Nickname:
The Empire State

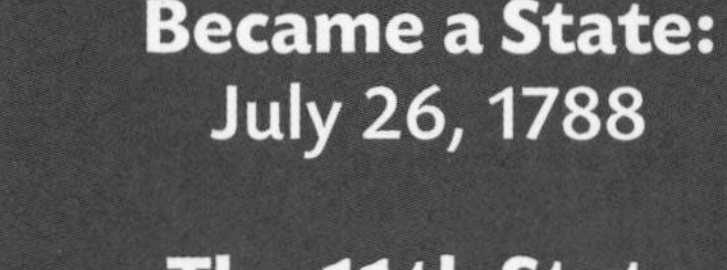

Fun Fact!

New York City is the largest city in the United States.

North Carolina

Find the correct sticker and place it here!

Became a State:
November 21, 1789

The 12th State

Capital:
Raleigh

State Nickname:
The Tar Heel State

Who invented and flew the first airplane?

Decode the letters to find out. Change each letter below to the one that comes after it in the alphabet.

V	Q	H	F	G	S

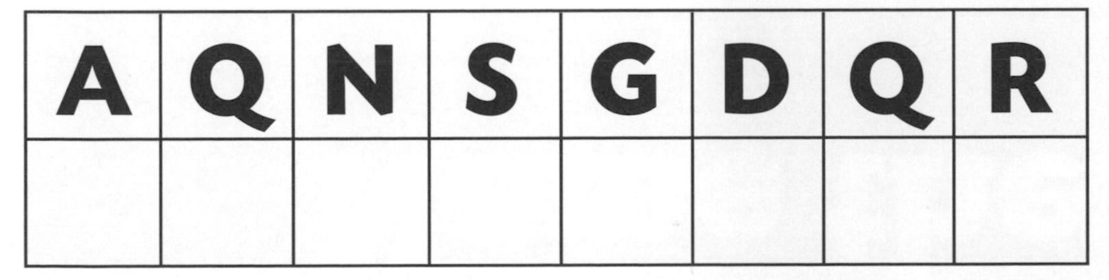

Turn to page 79 for the answer.

Fun Fact!

North Carolina produces more sweet potatoes than any other state.

Name the Country

What country gave the Statue of Liberty as a gift of friendship to the United States?

Use the code below to fill in the blanks and reveal the answer.

____ ____ ____ ____ ____ ____
3 9 26 7 25 24

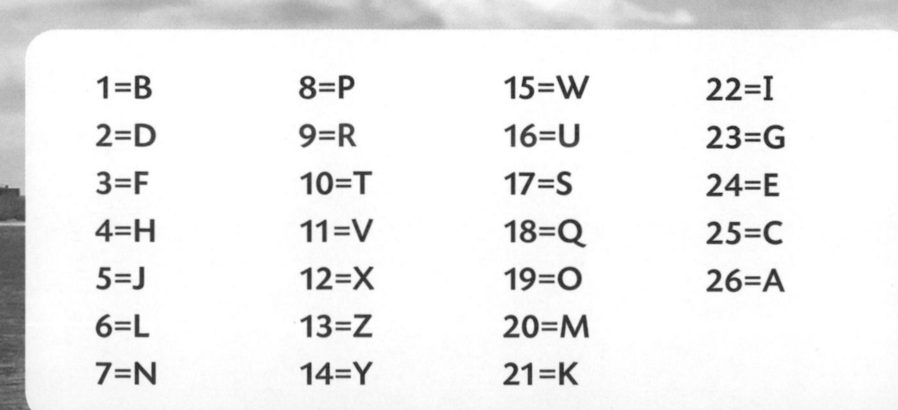

1=B	8=P	15=W	22=I
2=D	9=R	16=U	23=G
3=F	10=T	17=S	24=E
4=H	11=V	18=Q	25=C
5=J	12=X	19=O	26=A
6=L	13=Z	20=M	
7=N	14=Y	21=K	

Turn to page 79 for the answer.

North Dakota

Find the correct sticker and place it here!

The "World's Largest Buffalo" statue is located in Jamestown, North Dakota.

Circle the buffalo that is different from the others.

Turn to page 79 for the answer.

Became a State:
November 2, 1889

The 39th State

Capital:
Bismarck

State Nickname:
The Peace Garden State

Fun Fact!

Dakota is a Sioux word for "friends" or "allies."

Ohio

Find the correct sticker and place it here!

Ohio is home to which two halls of fame?

__ __ __ __   __   __ __ __ __
9 19 25 21   7   9 19 6 6

and

__ __ __ __ __ __ __ __
3 19 19 10 1 26 6 6

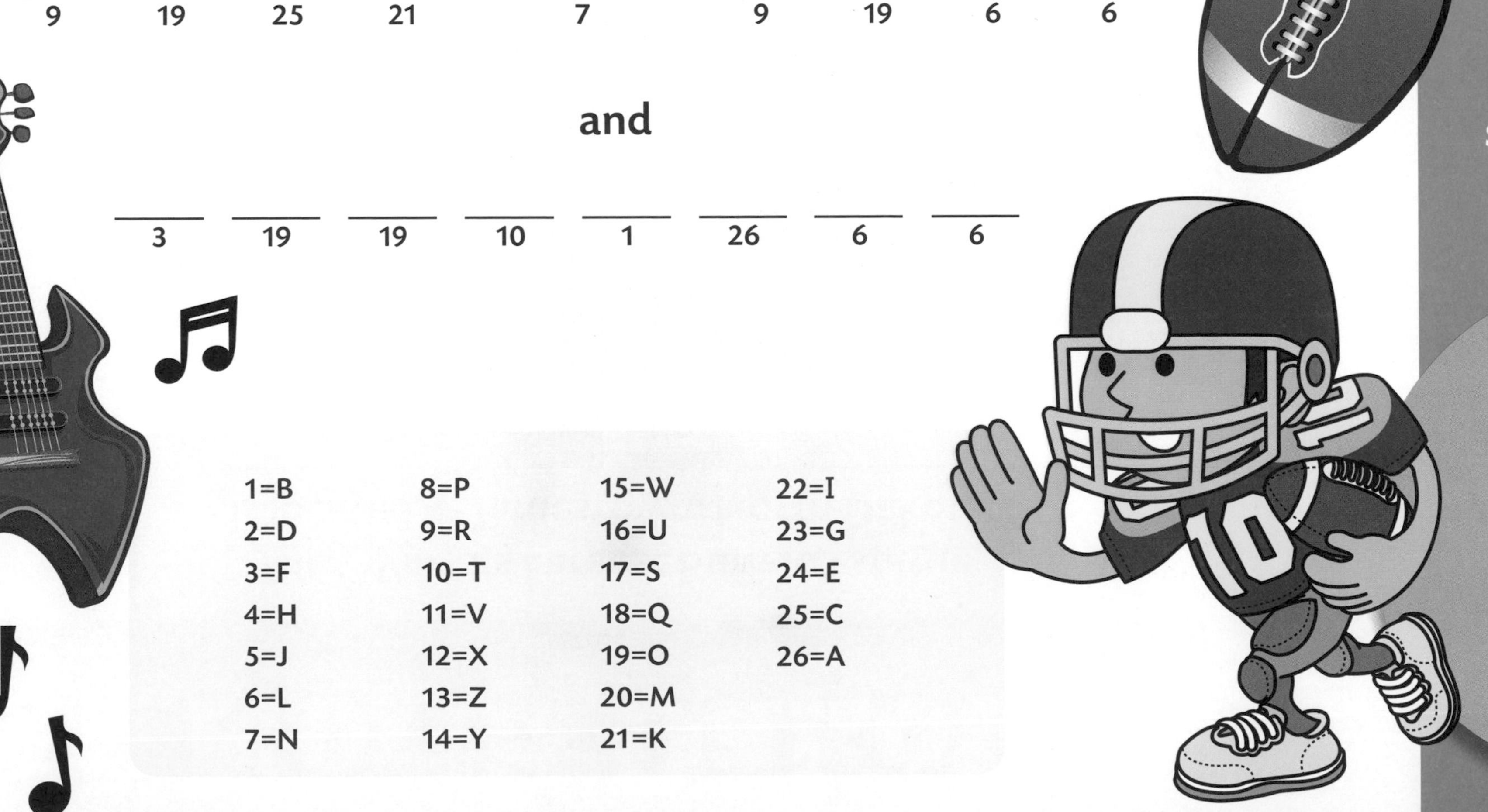

1=B	8=P	15=W	22=I
2=D	9=R	16=U	23=G
3=F	10=T	17=S	24=E
4=H	11=V	18=Q	25=C
5=J	12=X	19=O	26=A
6=L	13=Z	20=M	
7=N	14=Y	21=K	

Turn to page 79 for the answer.

Became a State:
March 1, 1803

The 17th State

Capital:
Columbus

State Nickname:
The Buckeye State

Fun Fact!

Ohio is an Iroquois word for "great river."

Here are two fun games you can play with family and friends when traveling on long road trips!

THE LICENSE PLATE GAME

Try and spot license plates from as many of the 50 states as you can. The person who finds the most wins! To score points, you have to be the first person to see the plate.

THE ROAD SIGN GAME

Try to spot these signs on the road. If you find one, you score! The player with the most points at the end of the trip is the winner.

- Stop Sign – 1 Point
- Wrong Way – 1 Point
- One Way – 1 Point
- Keep Right – 2 Points
- Speed Limit – 1 Point
- Rough Road – 3 Points
- Road Work Ahead – 2 Points
- Detour – 2 Points
- No Parking – 1 Point
- Bump – 2 Points
- Slippery When Wet – 3 Points
- Dip – 2 Points
- Deer Crossing – 2 Points
- Dead End – 2 Points
- No U-Turn – 2 Points
- Cattle Crossing – 2 Points
- Do Not Enter – 1 Point
- Slow – 1 Point
- Reserved Parking – 1 Point
- Tow Away Zone – 2 Points

Oklahoma

Find the correct sticker and place it here!

The National Cowboy Hall of Fame is located in Oklahoma City.

Circle the items that you would take with you for a day at the rodeo.

Became a State:
November 16, 1907

The 46th State

Capital:
Oklahoma City

State Nickname:
The Sooner State

Fun Fact!

The state bird is the scissor-tailed flycatcher.

Oregon

Find the correct sticker and place it here!

Help this beaver get back to his home.

Became a State:
February 14, 1859

The 33rd State

Capital:
Salem

State Nickname:
The Beaver State

Fun Fact!

Oregon's state animal is the beaver.

Turn to page 79 for the answer.

Name the Building

The president lives here.
The president's office–the Oval Office–is located here.
The building's address is 1600 Pennsylvania Avenue.

Use the code below to fill in the blanks
and reveal the answer.

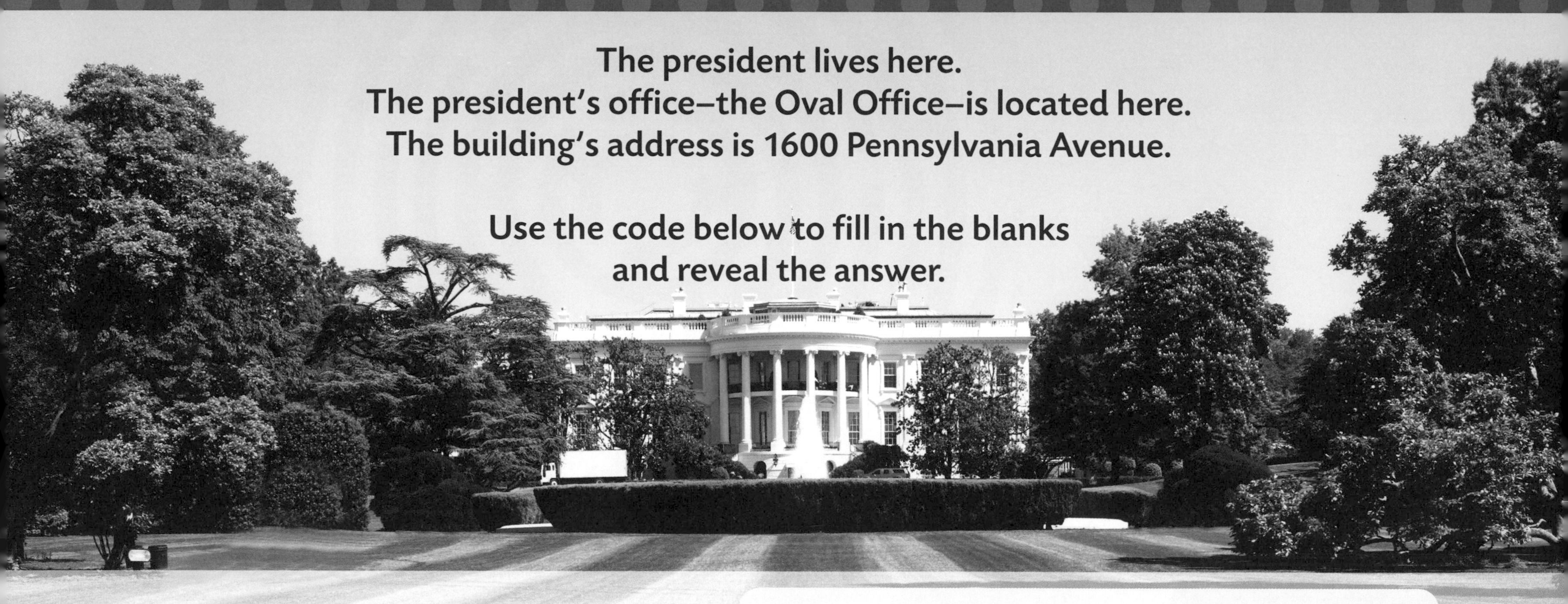

___ ___ ___ ___ ___
15 4 22 10 24

___ ___ ___ ___ ___
4 19 16 17 24

1=B	7=N	13=Z	19=O	25=C
2=D	8=P	14=Y	20=M	26=A
3=F	9=R	15=W	21=K	
4=H	10=T	16=U	22=I	
5=J	11=V	17=S	23=G	
6=L	12=X	18=Q	24=E	

Turn to page 79 for the answer.

Pennsylvania

Find the correct sticker and place it here!

On July 4, 1776, the Declaration of Independence was approved in this building.

Use the code below to fill in the blanks and reveal the answer.

___ ___ ___ ___ ___ ___ ___ ___ ___ ___ ___ ___
22 7 2 24 8 24 7 2 24 7 25 24

___ ___ ___ ___
4 26 6 6

1=B	10=T	19=O
2=D	11=V	20=M
3=F	12=X	21=K
4=H	13=Z	22=I
5=J	14=Y	23=G
6=L	15=W	24=E
7=N	16=U	25=C
8=P	17=S	26=A
9=R	18=Q	

Turn to page 79 for the answer.

Became a State:
December 12, 1787

The 2nd State

Capital:
Harrisburg

State Nickname:
The Keystone State

Fun Fact!

Pennsylvania produces more mushrooms than any other state.

Rhode Island

Find the correct sticker and place it here!

Rhode Island is the smallest state.

Circle the smallest item in each group.

Turn to page 79 for the answers.

Became a State:
May 29, 1790

The 13th State

Capital:
Providence

State Nickname:
The Ocean State

Fun Fact!

The first circus in the United States took place in Rhode Island.

South Carolina

Find the correct sticker and place it here!

South Carolina's eastern border is the Atlantic Ocean.

Color in the sand castle.

Became a State:
May 23, 1788

The 8th State

Capital:
Columbia

State Nickname:
The Palmetto State

Fun Fact!

The official state amphibian of South Carolina is the spotted salamander.

South Dakota

Find the correct sticker and place it here!

This is one of America's favorite monuments—Mount Rushmore. George Washington, Thomas Jefferson, and Theodore Roosevelt are three of the presidents featured. Use the code to fill in the blanks and reveal the remaining president.

___	___	___	___	___	___	___
26	1	9	26	4	26	20

___	___	___	___	___	___	___
6	22	7	25	19	6	7

1=B	4=H	7=N	10=T	13=Z	16=U	19=O	22=I	25=C
2=D	5=J	8=P	11=V	14=Y	17=S	20=M	23=G	26=A
3=F	6=L	9=R	12=X	15=W	18=Q	21=K	24=E	

Turn to page 79 for the answer.

Became a State:
November 2, 1889

The 40th State

Capital:
Pierre

State Nickname:
The Mount Rushmore State

Fun Fact!

The sculptures of Mount Rushmore are 60 feet tall.

Hangman

To play, one player thinks of a word and draws a dash for each letter of the word. The other player(s) guess the letters. If a correct letter is suggested, the first player writes it wherever it occurs in the word. For every incorrect letter guessed, the first player draws a body part of the hangman. And they keep track of the incorrect letters, so they are not used again. The game ends when a player guesses all the letters or the whole word correctly, or when the hangman drawing is completed.

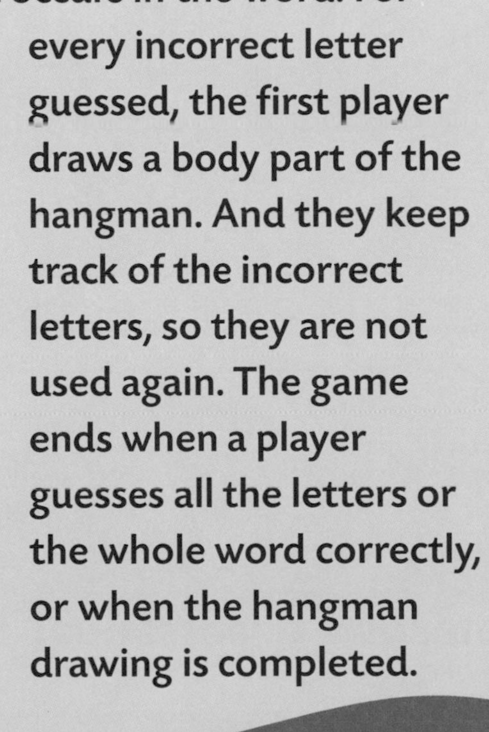

Tennessee

Find the
correct sticker
and place it here!

Nashville, Tennessee, is also known as "Music City."

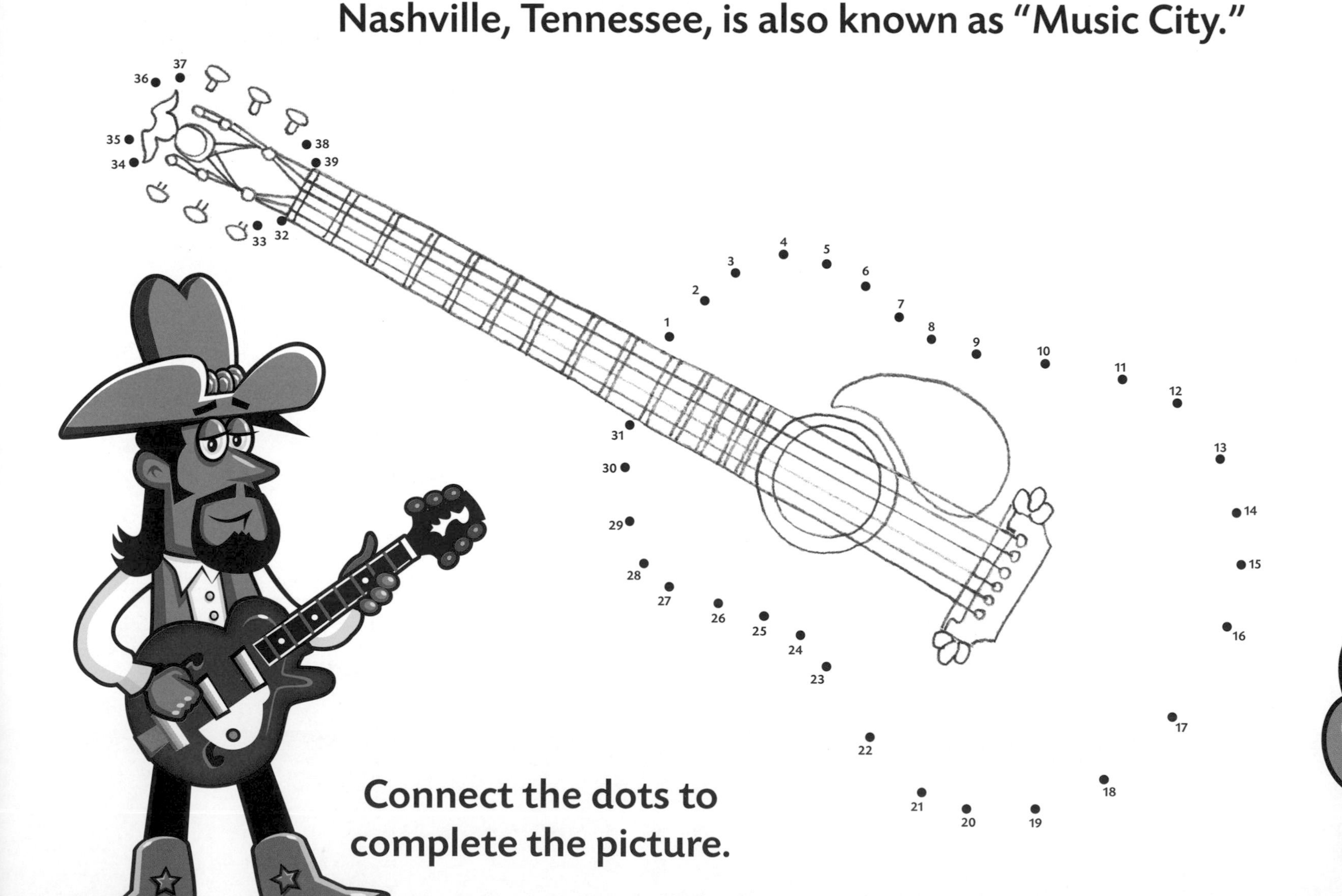

Connect the dots to
complete the picture.

Became a State:
June 1, 1796

The 15th State

Capital:
Nashville

State Nickname:
The Volunteer
State

Fun Fact!

Cotton candy was invented in Tennessee. It used to be called "fairy floss."

Texas

Find the correct sticker and place it here!

Davy Crockett fought in this famous battle.

Use the code below to fill in the blanks and reveal the answer.

___ ___ ___   ___ ___ ___ ___ ___

10 4 24   26 6 26 20 19

1=B	5=J	9=R	13=Z	17=S	21=K	25=C
2=D	6=L	10=T	14=Y	18=Q	22=I	26=A
3=F	7=N	11=V	15=W	19=O	23=G	
4=H	8=P	12=X	16=U	20=M	24=E	

Turn to page 79 for the answer.

Became a State:
December 29, 1845

The 28th State

Capital:
Austin

State Nickname:
The Lone Star State

Fun Fact!

Texas produces more cotton than any other state.

Utah

Find the correct sticker and place it here!

Salt Lake City

UTAH

Utah has lots of ski resorts. The 2002 Winter Olympics were held in Salt Lake City, Utah.

Draw a line from the skier on the left that matches the skier on the right.

Turn to page 80 for the answers.

Became a State:
January 4, 1896

The 44th State

Capital:
Salt Lake City

State Nickname:
The Beehive State

Fun Fact!

Utah's Great Salt Lake is so salty, you can float in it.

Welcome to the Southwest!
Use the stickers in the front of the book
to create a fun desert scene.

Vermont

Find the correct sticker and place it here!

Montpelier

VERMONT

Find the picture of the maple leaves that is different from the others.

A

B

C

D

Turn to page 80 for the answer.

Became a State:
March 4, 1791

The 14th State

Capital:
Montpelier

State Nickname:
The Green Mountain State

Fun Fact!

Vermont makes more maple syrup than any other state.

Virginia

Find the correct sticker and place it here!

Virginia is the birthplace of seven U.S. presidents, including the one pictured on the right.

Use the code below to fill in the blanks and reveal the answer.

___ ___ ___ ___ ___ ___
10 4 19 20 26 17

___ ___ ___ ___ ___ ___ ___ ___ ___
5 24 3 3 24 9 17 19 7

1=B	5=J	9=R	13=Z	17=S	21=K	25=C
2=D	6=L	10=T	14=Y	18=Q	22=I	26=A
3=F	7=N	11=V	15=W	19=O	23=G	
4=H	8=P	12=X	16=U	20=M	24=E	

Became a State:
June 25, 1788

The 10th State

Capital:
Richmond

State Nickname:
Old Dominion

Fun Fact!

Jamestown, Virginia, was the first English settlement in America.

Turn to page 80 for the answer.

Match the road signs with the correct message.

1. ____________

2. ____________

3. ____________

4. ____________

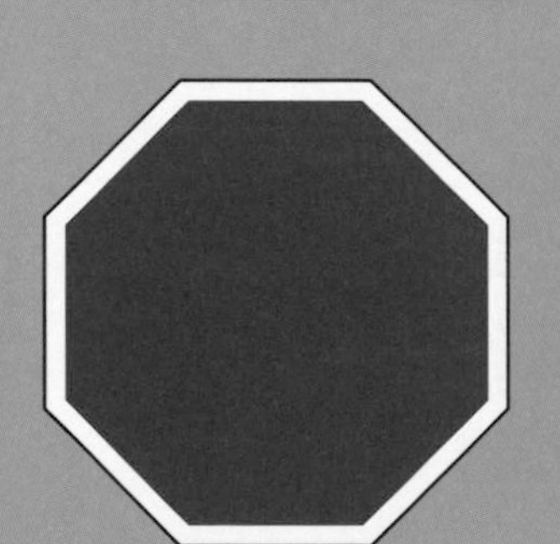

5. ____________

6. ____________

7. ____________

8. ____________

9. ____________

Railroad Crossing

Speed Limit

Stop

Fire Truck Crossing

Yield

School Zone

Double Bend

Do Not Enter

No Parking

Turn to page 80 for the answers.

Washington

Find the correct sticker and place it here!

See if you can find the words listed below in the word search. They can be found forward, backward, and diagonally.

Seattle

Salmon

Space Needle

Raspberries

Mount St. Helens

Evergreens

Turn to page 80 for the answers.

Became a State:
November 11, 1889

The 42nd State

Capital:
Olympia

State Nickname:
The Evergreen State

Fun Fact!

Washington is the only state that is named after a president.

West Virginia

Find the correct sticker and place it here!

Charleston

WEST VIRGINIA

West Virginia is the nation's leading producer of underground coal.

Help the miner find the coal.

Turn to page 80 for the answer.

Became a State:
June 20, 1863

The 35th State

Capital:
Charleston

State Nickname:
The Mountain State

Fun Fact!

West Virginia is called the "southernmost northern state" and the "northermost southern state."

Wisconsin

Find the correct sticker and place it here!

Wisconsin is known as "the Dairy Capital of the United States." It produces more milk than any other state.

Circle the two cows that are identical.

Turn to page 80 for the answer.

Became a State:
May 29, 1848

The 30th State

Capital:
Madison

State Nickname:
The Badger State

Fun Fact!

Wisconsin produces more cheese than any other state.

Wyoming

Find the correct sticker and place it here!

Cheyenne

WYOMING

What is the name of this famous geyser in Yellowstone National Park in Wyoming?

Decode the letters to find out. Change each letter below to the one that comes before it in the alphabet.

P	M	E

G	B	J	U	I	E	V	M

Turn to page 80 for the answer.

Became a State:
July 10, 1890

The 44th State

Capital:
Cheyenne

State Nickname:
The Equality State

Fun Fact!

Wyoming's state dinosaur is the Triceratops.

Welcome to Yellowstone National Park!
Use the stickers in the front of the book
to create an animal-filled scene.

Washington, D.C.

See if you can find the words listed below in the word search. They can be found forward, backward, and diagonally.

S	Q	W	X	A	T	N	E	M	U	N	O	M	N	O	T	G	N	I	H	S	A	W
U	R	U	K	R	L	D	R	K	R	W	X	V	R	B	C	G	T	E	M	V	U	X
P	K	P	J	V	Z	R	P	Q	F	S	V	U	X	C	Q	T	K	I	U	H	K	G
R	U	N	A	T	I	O	N	A	L	G	A	L	L	E	R	Y	A	E	Q	T	P	V
E	I	U	J	D	P	W	G	H	P	Q	F	I	Q	X	C	M	A	Y	Y	S	K	W
M	Z	Z	B	H	U	H	O	Z	O	M	F	K	F	I	Z	K	W	U	S	F	H	T
E	Q	O	L	I	N	C	O	L	N	M	E	M	O	R	I	A	L	G	H	I	R	X
C	C	C	Y	T	F	R	U	A	U	I	G	V	X	A	P	I	Y	B	T	B	S	O
O	X	U	D	A	O	J	D	T	V	W	P	Z	N	A	U	M	U	E	R	U	G	N
U	U	U	J	Y	I	D	N	Y	A	D	F	B	U	F	O	R	H	G	Q	V	D	X
R	Y	N	T	H	E	C	A	P	I	T	O	L	K	E	N	O	F	S	S	U	X	R
T	C	B	B	D	N	U	T	X	Q	Y	Z	D	L	T	U	H	R	B	M	X	G	J
F	K	L	R	L	C	C	R	X	H	F	Q	L	P	S	O	V	Z	I	L	O	P	D
M	C	O	P	A	G	I	P	J	O	P	M	B	E	Y	P	A	Q	S	Y	D	J	L

White House

Washington Monument

Lincoln Memorial

Supreme Court

National Gallery

The Capitol

Turn to page 80 for the answers.

The District of Columbia is the capital of the United States.

It became the nation's capital on June 11, 1800.

Many government buildings are located here, such as the White House, the Capitol, and the Supreme Court.

Use the star stickers in the front of the book to show where you have traveled, or to map out your dream road trip across the United States.

Name the Capital

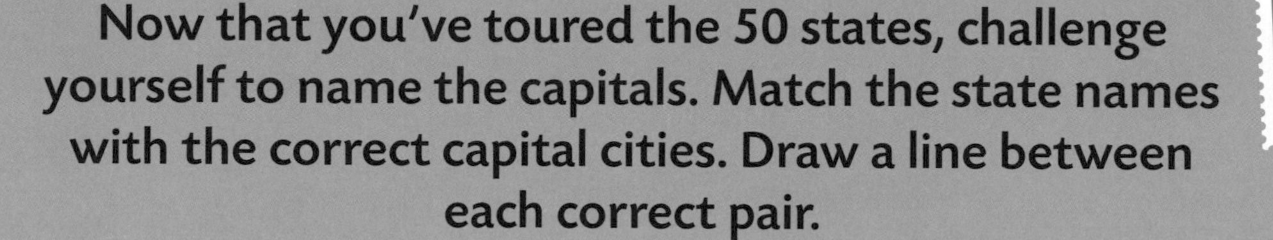

Now that you've toured the 50 states, challenge yourself to name the capitals. Match the state names with the correct capital cities. Draw a line between each correct pair.

STATES	CAPITALS	STATES	CAPITALS
Alabama	Little Rock	Hawaii	Indianapolis
Alaska	Sacramento	Idaho	Honolulu
Arizona	Montgomery	Illinois	Boise
Arkansas	Juneau	Indiana	Des Moines
California	Phoenix	Iowa	Springfield
Colorado	Atlanta	Kansas	Frankfort
Connecticut	Tallahassee	Kentucky	Augusta
Delaware	Denver	Louisiana	Topeka
Florida	Hartford	Maine	Annapolis
Georgia	Dover	Maryland	Baton Rouge

Turn to page 80 for the answers.

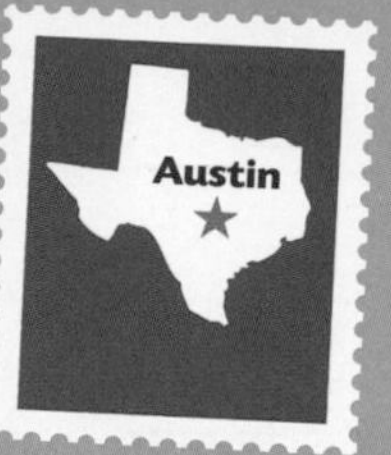

STATES	CAPITALS	STATES	CAPITALS
Massachusetts	St. Paul	Oklahoma	Harrisburg
Michigan	Jackson	Oregon	Providence
Minnesota	Lansing	Pennsylvania	Salem
Mississippi	Jefferson City	Rhode Island	Oklahoma City
Missouri	Boston	South Carolina	Columbia
Montana	Helena	South Dakota	Austin
Nebraska	Concord	Tennessee	Montpelier
Nevada	Trenton	Texas	Pierre
New Hampshire	Lincoln	Utah	Nashville
New Jersey	Carson City	Vermont	Salt Lake City
New Mexico	Bismarck	Virginia	Madison
New York	Columbus	Washington	Richmond
North Carolina	Santa Fe	West Virginia	Olympia
North Dakota	Albany	Wisconsin	Cheyenne
Ohio	Raleigh	Wyoming	Charleston

Turn to page 80 for the answers.

My Travels

Famous places I have seen:

I have been to these states:

Some of the cool things I have seen when traveling:

States/places I'd like to visit:

Answer Key

Page 3

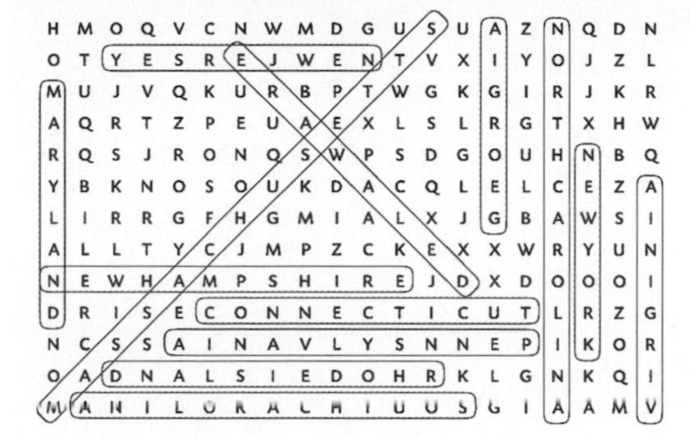

Page 4

GEORGE WASHINGTON

Page 6

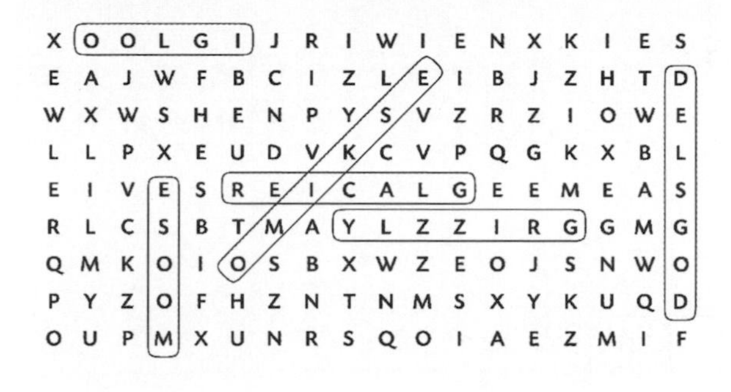

Page 7

Page 8

Q	Z	Y	N	Q	A	Z	B	J
R	A	Z	O	R	B	A	C	K

Page 9

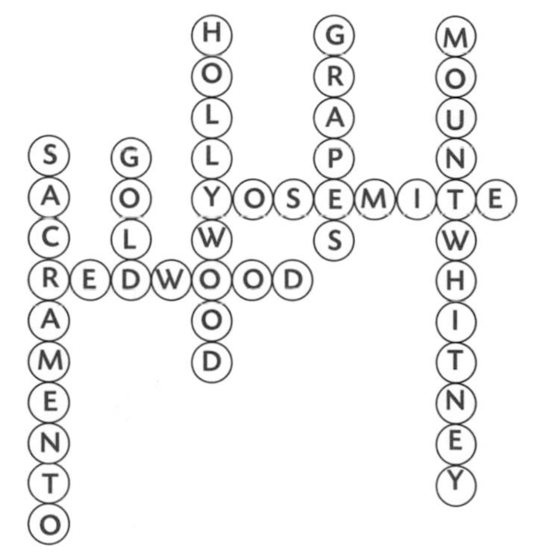

Page 10

1. To the beach
2. Tennis pro
3. Never late
4. You are pretty
5. Need for speed
6. Road warrior
7. Are you for real?
8. Wait for me
9. Excuse me
10. Speed demon

Page 13

PEACH BLOSSOM

Page 14

Page 16

Page 17

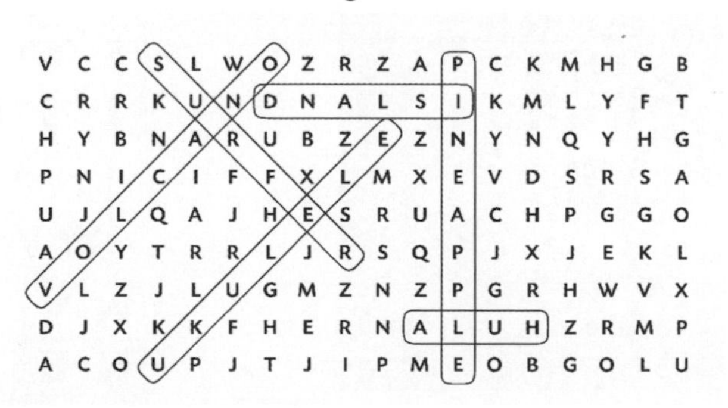

Page 19

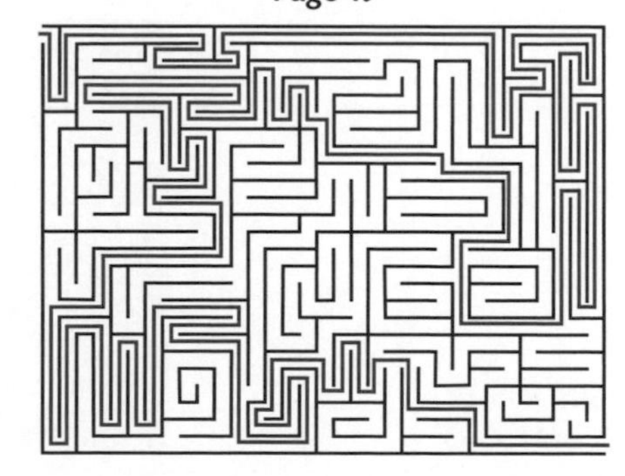

Page 20

WILLISTOWER
CHICAGO
PRAIRIESTATE
SPRINGFIELD
LINCOLN
JANEADDAMS

Page 22

J		B	N
I		A	M

B	M	M
A	L	L

F	B	S	T
E	A	R	S

Page 24

C

Page 26

ABRAHAM
LINCOLN

Page 27

R K C C X L P U U G U C T E N Z N I N Q
B H N J E C H J Y F N O H C D U E I B M
U A R Y H U G D P W S N Y V Q Q W O A P
B R T A C C B V F J B R B A K P O P F X
L Q C T L S A R G I D R A M B E R Y W R
Y G T F Y L V C B A A O N S S L L G J H
J R I C C H I G I B Y B I V Y I E U A B
G I K S W V B G Z F F Y F A B C A D Z J
P K L F Y X P U A Z E I Y I P A N K Z F
D O K I W A N C X T D Y R N G N S U R U
T D W O K G Q S N V O V B K P S E V O A
A U T O K X V N A M V R Y S S P S W B O

Page 28

Page 29

Page 30

N	Q	H	N	K	D	R
O	R	I	O	L	E	S

Page 31

PILGRIMS

Page 32

SUPERIOR
MICHIGAN
ONTARIO
HURON
ERIE

Page 34

Page 35

H	B	U	F	R	B	Z
G	A	T	E	W	A	Y

B	S	D	I
A	R	C	H

Page 36

UNCLESAM
AMERICANFLAG
LIBERTYBELL
BALDEAGLE
MAYFLOWER
STATUEOFLIBERTY

Page 37

CRAZY HORSE

Page 39

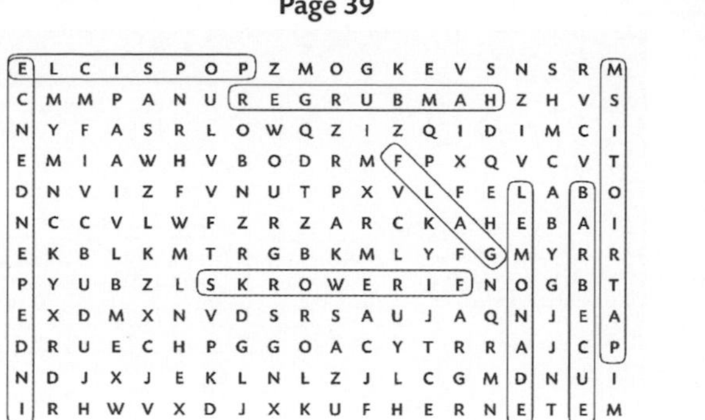

Page 40

Page 42

B E O F B J V E S A T N O H A C O P P Z C V
C Q J N H N I L K N A R F N I M A J N E B G
Q C W R A U B P P G W K S F Z P B E Y B B D
B N X Z R L E Z V G T S U D P P V L U P D T
I F Z L R I N C N Z O H H T R O R Y A H D I
M K Y A I F B U K R L K Z Z J I M T U P O C
F B S D E F B G Y R Z E R E V E R L U A P S
P F T H T W D S W J C I A B I I F X D K M K
S P H B T L T B N H G O D K C T K G B B D W
W R S A U E G R W G F S L K K Y L C W I V W
V W K A B X C G A P K F H V V P A Z V T Z N
T A Q F M L V R T V C E F K D U B D F V K I
T Q Y B A R G C A E N I C F F U T L U E Z K
A R W B N B E A I R I K P J C X Z B J T Y G
J U S A D U M Q Y M N X W S X D G V W L H J
S N I J A S S A L G U O D K C I R E D E R F
E E I L H Z P H J A N E A D D A M S M N Y Z

Page 43

THE BATTLE OF TRENTON

Page 46

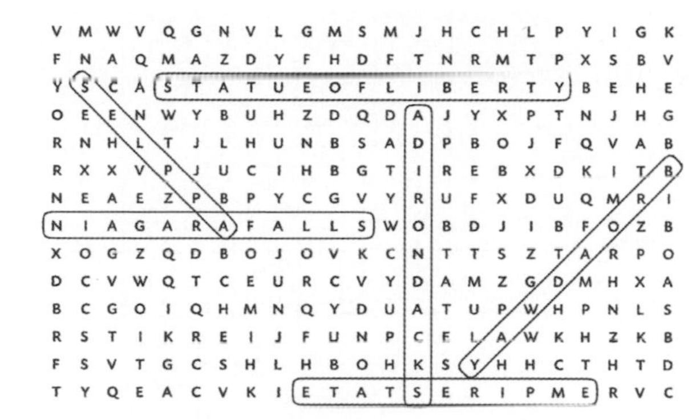

Page 47

V	Q	H	F	G	S
W	R	I	G	H	T

A	Q	N	S	G	D	Q	R
B	R	O	T	H	E	R	S

Page 48

FRANCE

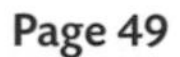

Page 49

Page 50

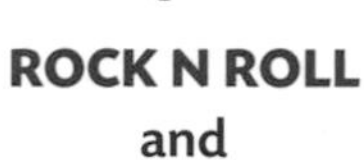

ROCK N ROLL and FOOTBALL

Page 53

Page 54

WHITE HOUSE

Page 55

INDEPENDENCE HALL

Page 56

Page 58

ABRAHAM LINCOLN

Page 61

THE ALAMO

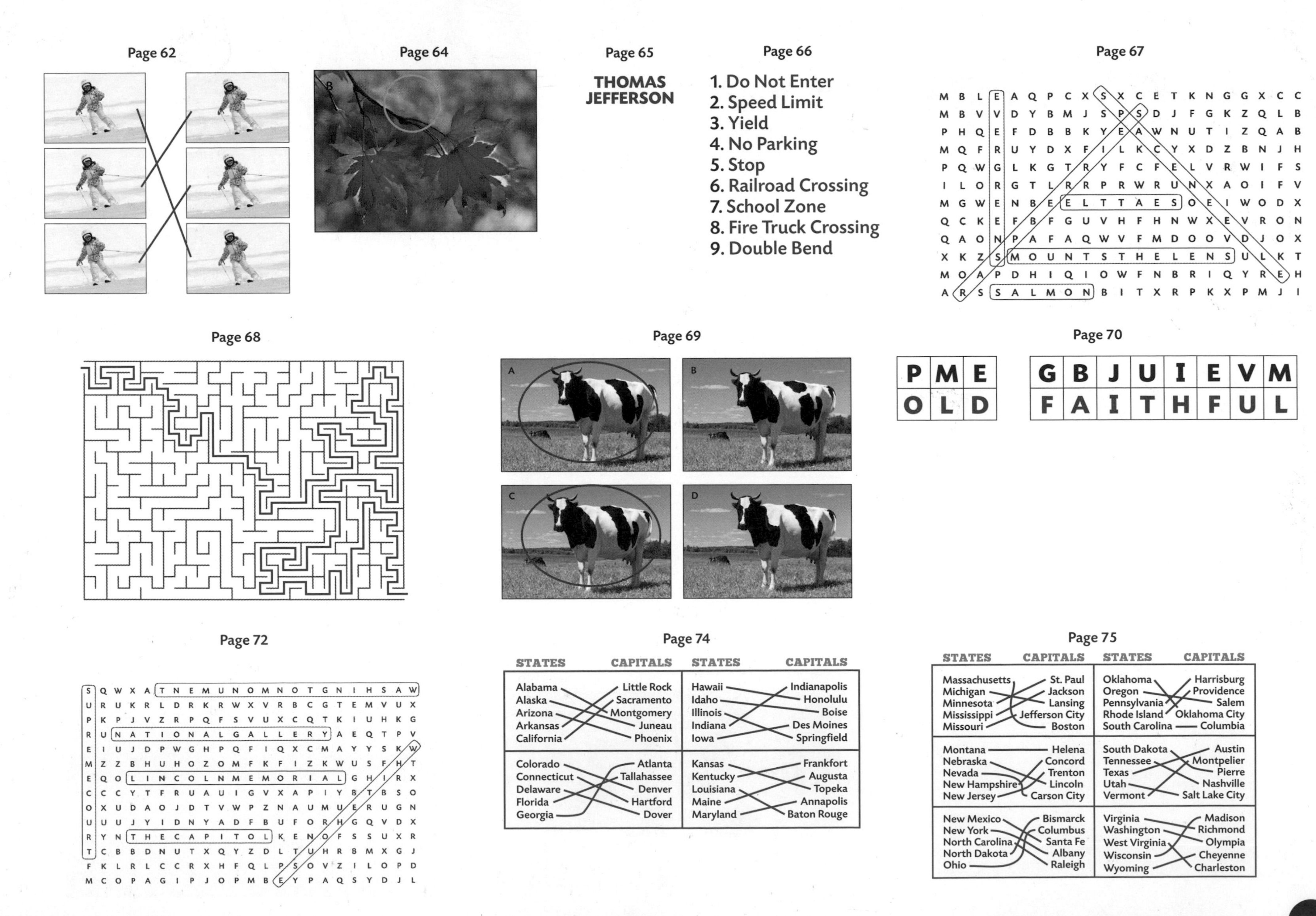
Page 62
Page 64
B
Page 65
THOMAS JEFFERSON
Page 66
1. Do Not Enter
2. Speed Limit
3. Yield
4. No Parking
5. Stop
6. Railroad Crossing
7. School Zone
8. Fire Truck Crossing
9. Double Bend
Page 67
Page 68
Page 69
A
B
C
D
Page 70
P M E
O L D
G B J U I E V M
F A I T H F U L
Page 72
Page 74
STATES CAPITALS STATES CAPITALS
Alabama Alaska Arizona Arkansas California
Little Rock Sacramento Montgomery Juneau Phoenix
Hawaii Idaho Illinois Indiana Iowa
Indianapolis Honolulu Boise Des Moines Springfield
Colorado Connecticut Delaware Florida Georgia
Atlanta Tallahassee Denver Hartford Dover
Kansas Kentucky Louisiana Maine Maryland
Frankfort Augusta Topeka Annapolis Baton Rouge
Page 75
STATES CAPITALS STATES CAPITALS
Massachusetts Michigan Minnesota Mississippi Missouri
St. Paul Jackson Lansing Jefferson City Boston
Oklahoma Oregon Pennsylvania Rhode Island South Carolina
Harrisburg Providence Salem Oklahoma City Columbia
Montana Nebraska Nevada New Hampshire New Jersey
Helena Concord Trenton Lincoln Carson City
South Dakota Tennessee Texas Utah Vermont
Austin Montpelier Pierre Nashville Salt Lake City
New Mexico New York North Carolina North Dakota Ohio
Bismarck Columbus Santa Fe Albany Raleigh
Virginia Washington West Virginia Wisconsin Wyoming
Madison Richmond Olympia Cheyenne Charleston